EVERYTHING®
C·R·A·F·T·S

Rubber Stamping

Made Easy

Step-by-Step Instructions for Creating Fun and Original Projects

Edited by Courtney Nolan

Adams Media
Avon, Massachusetts

An Everything® Series Book.
Everything® and everything.com® are registered trademarks of F+W Publications, Inc.

Published by Adams Media, an F+W Publications Company
57 Littlefield Street, Avon, MA 02322 U.S.A.
www.adamsmedia.com

ISBN: 1-59337-229-9
Printed in the United States of America.

J I H G F E D C B A

Library of Congress Cataloging-in-Publication Data
Everything crafts—rubber stamping made easy / edited by Courtney Nolan.
p.   cm. — (An everything series book)
ISBN 1-59337-229-9
1. Rubber stamp printing. I. Nolan, Courtney. II. Series: Everything series.

TT867.E94 2004
761--dc22

2004013572

This publication is designed to provide accurate and authoritative information with regard to the subject matter covered. It is sold with the understanding that the publisher is not engaged in rendering legal, accounting, or other professional advice. If legal advice or other expert assistance is required, the services of a competent professional person should be sought.
—From a *Declaration of Principles* jointly adopted by a Committee of the American Bar Association and a Committee of Publishers and Associations

Many of the designations used by manufacturers and sellers to distinguish their products are claimed as trademarks. Where those designations appear in this book and Adams Media was aware of a trademark claim, the designations have been printed with initial capital letters.

This book is available at quantity discounts for bulk purchases.
For information, call 1-800-872-5627.

Some material in this publication has been adapted and compiled
from the following previously published works:

McCall, Sandra	*Making Gifts with Rubber Stamps* ©2000 (F+W Publications, Inc.)
Abel, Vesta	*Rubber Stamp Extravaganza* ©2001 (F+W Publications, Inc.)
McCall, Sandra	*30-Minute Rubber Stamp Workshop* ©2002 (F+W Publications, Inc.)

All works of art reproduced in this book have been previously copyrighted by the individual artists.
The designs herein may not be resold or republished.

Photography by: Christine Polomsky and Al Parrish

Table of Contents

Part III • 87
Extra Credit Fun

Welcome to the *Everything® Crafts* Series!

If you want to get in touch with your inner creativity but aren't sure where to begin, you've already completed Step One—choosing the perfect resource to help you get started. THE EVERYTHING® CRAFTS books are ideal for beginners because they provide illustrated, step-by-step instruction for creating fun—and unique—projects.

THE EVERYTHING® CRAFTS books bring the craft world back to the basics, providing easy-to-follow direction on finding appropriate tools and materials to learn new craft techniques. These clear and readable books guide you every step of the way from beginning until end, teaching you tips and tricks to get your craft to look just right.

So sit back and enjoy. This experience is all about introducing you to the world of crafts—and, most of all, learning EVERYTHING you can!

A note to our readers:

We are delighted to bring to you tons of fun rubber-stamping projects to experiment with, create, and have a blast crafting! Choose to create anything from adorable miniature boxes to classy pin accessories to elegant lampshades. There is a little something creative for everyone to take part in with the *Everything® Crafts—Rubber Stamping Made Easy* book. Remember, rubber stamps are to be used as additional tools to enhance and shape your art—so whether it's a project that requires one stamp, or a project that asks for many, you're in control of what you create—so don't let anyone stop you or tell you how to be an artist!

This book would not be possible without the hard work and effort from many, especially: Jane Friedman and everyone at North Light Books, Christine Polomsky and Al Parrish, and artists everywhere who inspired the projects that are included in this book.

Also, a very special thank you to the fantastic rubber stamp companies who created the stamps used in the projects here.

—The Editors, EVERYTHING® CRAFTS *Series*

Introduction

Have you always wanted to be creative? Do you want to use your hands to craft beautiful works of art and be that person who presents the crafts you make to friends and family as gifts? You can with this book! All you need is some time, patience, and an open mind, and you too can create the glorious crafts in this book.

The projects in *Everything® Crafts—Rubber Stamping Made Easy* are for you, the beginner. You are not to be discouraged or frustrated when the first few tries yield projects that do not look perfect. Have no fear. With time and good energy, you'll be creating works of art that won't be explained to you on the following pages because you'll have mastered your own rubber-stamping techniques. What follows in this book are instructions and visuals that serve only as a foundation of what is yet to come—using your imagination to create projects of your own. Hopefully you'll share your discoveries with other fellow artists.

Read the first section to get a good understanding about the materials and tools that are handy to have nearby so that you don't have to stop and run to the store because you've run out of ink in the middle of a project.

The crafts aren't in a special order—flip to a page with a project you think looks marvelous and get going—there is no such thing as "too hard" or "too complicated." Get crafty!

★ ★ ★ ★ ★

Part I

Rubber Stamping Is Easy: What You Need to Know

Tools & Materials

First things first: You can't get anywhere without knowing the fundamentals about rubber stamping, but don't worry, we'll keep this short. These next few pages will list various materials that are important to have in your possession so that when you flip to any project, you'll have most of the items asked for on hand. Each materials section is labeled as *Must-Haves: Materials,* so remember to pay attention to that even if you have a wide collection of stamps and inks and think you're all set to begin.

Stamping 101

Listed below are the nuts and bolts of stamping. Read on for lots more info and stamp away!

Stamps

Rule #1: The deeper the etching on a rubber stamp, the better quality the stamp. A deeper image will allow better depth for stamping on clay, a better impression for stamping on fabric, and will stand up better to a variety of other materials.

Purchase unmounted stamps (a stamp that is just rubber—no wood or cushion) through the mail, at conventions, online, or at rubber stamp stores. Stamps can be stored in three-ring binders in pocket holders or in sheet protectors.

There are a variety of mounting methods for unmounted stamps. One way is to use double-stick tape between a block of acrylic and the unmounted stamp. If you have a large, unmounted stamp that does not stamp clearly, add a cushion by attaching a layer of fun foam to the back of the unmounted stamp with rubber cement.

Inks

Use the proper ink for your project so that you experience stamping success. Try **Décor-it** inks for your projects. They are quick-drying and permanent. You can also try **Adirondack** dye-based inks. These are good for paper-dying and for staining gourds. **Fabrico** pigment inks are also a nice choice as they are a "one size fits all" ink for a beginner. With Fabrico, you can emboss and shrink wrap with them. They are permanent when heat set and give off lovely

effects on metals. They are ideal for staining papier-mâché items and good for stenciling on walls because they wash off well if you make a mistake.

Tips & Quips: Not sure which ink to use? If you want a quick-drying ink for paper, use dye-based inks. If you want quick-drying ink that is also waterproof, use **Décor-it**—apply it with a makeup sponge. **Fabrico** inks are only waterproof when heat set. So choose your inks according to your needs and wants.

Heat Tool or Heat Gun

A must have! This tool is indispensable—it is great for embossing safely, but you can also use it to shrink plastic, heat foam, and set inks. Some good brands are **Ranger's Heat-it**. This one never gets too hot. It's quiet and easy to hold and it won't blow embossing powder all over. Its large heating area makes heating foam and candles a cinch.

Paintbrushes

Purchase an inexpensive, disposable brush with a feathered tip so that you can texture your cards with paint, ink, and bleach. A large, soft camel-hair paintbrush works well to brush off excess embossing powder. Foam brushes are good for smoothing on paste for paste paper or for applying aged-metal products such as rust and green patinas. Have a variety of brushes on hand for any watercolor or other painting you'll want to do.

Paper

There are various types of paper that are asked for in this book: chipboard, text-weight, hand-dyed, hand-made, paper wood, cardstock, etc. It's important you use the correct type of paper that the project asks for so that you can achieve the same successful results. Consult your local craft store for more advice about paper and any experimentation you may engage in. Here are a few words on some of the types to get you started:

- **Chipboard:** inexpensive, multipurpose material, art supply stores usually carry **Davey Board**, which is an acid-free white coated paper—it is more expensive than regular chipboard

- **Text-weight:** lighter than chipboard, used for interior pages of book projects, used also to wrap chipboard covers and boxes

- **Cardstock:** stiffer, heavier paper used for card and small gift box crafts

Embossing Powders

These powders can be applied in many ways. You can shake them onto images stamped in pigment inks or onto pigment ink applied directly to the paper, or onto strips of double-stick tape.

Tips & Quips: Embossing is an easy task. Stamp your design using a pigment or dye-based ink, sprinkle embossing powder over it, tap off any excess, and heat until design is shiny and bonds to the paper.

Cutting Must-Haves

To cut and punch lots of objects in order to create most of the projects in this book, you'll need to have on hand a craft knife, hole punch, wire cutters, and scissors.

Shrink Plastic

Shrink plastic is something that is useful when creating buttons, pins, jewelry, charms, and other accessories. It comes in varied colors and thicknesses. It is easiest to use a heat tool with shrink plastic, but an oven is a good alternative too.

Glues and Adhesives

Products like **Almost Leather** and **Metal Quilting** need special glues to attach them to other surfaces. A spray adhesive like **Super 77** by **3M** is excellent for these products and for paper. It leaves no ripples in paper and dries quite fast. Double-sided foam tape is a good alternative when you want a raised dimension to your project. **Jewel Bond** is great for adhering beads and other large or heavy embellishments to surfaces.

Brayer

A good brayer is one from **Ranger Industries**—it is made from solid material so that you can burn designs into it with a wood burner to make your very own rolling stamp! It also has little feet on the sides so that it keeps inks and paints away from your workspace when you set it down.

Awl

Use this for punching holes into items like chipboard, leather, or a stack of papers to be stab bound.

Pin Vise

Available at hobby shops, it is a handle with different sized chucks to hold a variety of small drill bits. You can easily drill through anything simply by turning the pin vise like a screwdriver. Use it on chipboard, polymer clay, and paperclay, and to drill beads that need a larger hole.

Utility and Craft Knives

Utility knives cut chipboard or mat board. Craft knives are good for cutting papers and for scoring chipboard.

Stylus

Having a stylus or two that differ in size is a good idea. These are handy for dry embossing on paper and for scoring paper and chipboard. You can also use a stylus to mark soft clay.

Cutting Mat

Purchase a quality mat that is self healing and has grid marks that are easy to read. Remember, do not use your heat gun on your cutting mat!

Tips & Quips: For the stamps that need cushioning under the paper so that you can stamp a clear image, try using a computer mouse pad—it works quite well!

Penscore

This is a type of foam that works wonders for creating your own texture stamps. Reheat it and you can take the old design off and mold a new one!

Almost Leather

This is a foam product that looks and feels like leather when it is heated. It is applied with permanent inks for decoration.

Metal Quilting

This is real copper sheeting that is used with a stylus or pen.

Gold Leaf

This is an amazingly thin foil that is wonderful for many things. It is fantastic when paired with clay, tape, frames, foam—you name it!

Dyna Vinyl

This and other static cling vinyls work well for the stained-glass look type projects. They also make great decals that you can embellish glassware with.

Clay

Air dry and oven bake clays are fun to get your hands into. Polymer clay is oven baked in order to harden and last properly. It comes in a variety of brands and how hard or soft it is depends on the brand. Air dry clay requires no oven time. It is lighter than polymer clay, but less durable.

Dimensional Magic

A clear liquid which comes in many colors, this is wonderful to add for a raised look on cards, wood, metal, and plastic. It takes a while to dry, but if you use a heat tool, you can speed up the process. Watch out, because the liquid can bubble when heated!

Plastic Sheets

Acrylic, styrene, and Plexiglas fall under the plastics category. If you purchase Plexiglas or acrylic, you will need to buy a plastic cutter. Thin styrene is probably most desirable to use because it can be cut and trimmed with long-bladed tin snips or an old pair of heavy-duty scissors. To make holes, you can use a small Fiskars hand drill or pin vise.

Other Accessories

Use beads, stones, gems, threads, tassels, wires, and anything else to jazz up and beautify your projects. Old keys, watch or clock parts, thrift store finds, buttons, charms, anything lying around the house—these are all wonderful ways to add to your projects and make them more you and more unique!

Unique Techniques

★ **Now that you have** a basic understanding of some of the products and tools you'll need to make your life easier when you start creating rubber stamp crafts, it's time to explain how to go about creating your own stamp, getting the best rubber stamp looks, and how to get your feet wet in this craft before you start your first official project!

Create a Stamp: Method One

This is one of two methods you can use to make your own stamp. If you are sick of the texture stamp you first create, simply heat the foam and create another with any other object.

Must-Haves: Materials

Penscore foam block • Heat tool • Objects with texture: basket, raffia, paper clip, shoe • Ink pad • Décor-it metallic inks (optional) • Paper

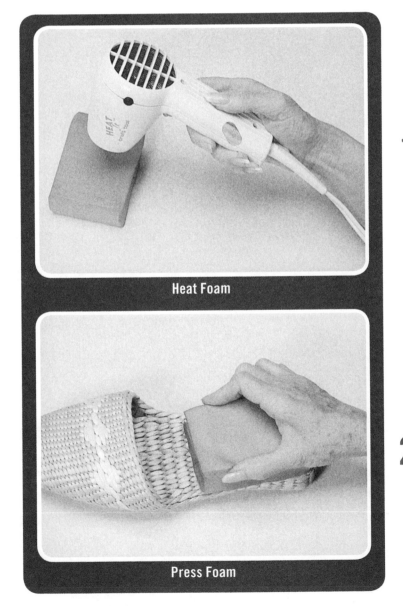

Heat Foam

Press Foam

1 Heat foam block until it gets soft, about 30 seconds.

2 Quickly press foam onto textured surface (in this case, a shoe).

3 Look at your stamp!

See Stamp

4 Ink stamp in pad and press firmly onto stamping surface.

Ink Stamp and Press onto Surface

5 Wipe the stamp off and reheat foam to remove old stamp design. Press foam on new surface to create a new stamp. Penscore can be heated multiple times.

Clean Stamp and Create New Design

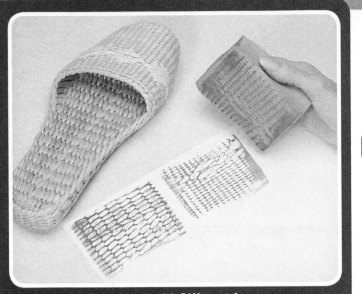

Experiment with Different Areas

6 Experiment with different areas on the same object.

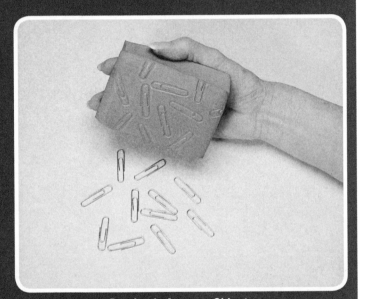

Randomly Arrange Objects

7 Randomly arrange objects for an interesting look.

Notice Light and Dark Areas

8 Light and dark areas create a striking look.

9 Ink the stamp, then remove some of the ink with a crumpled paper to achieve a batik look.

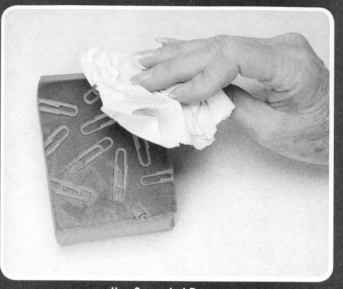

Use Crumpled Paper

10 Achieve two different looks from the same stamp.

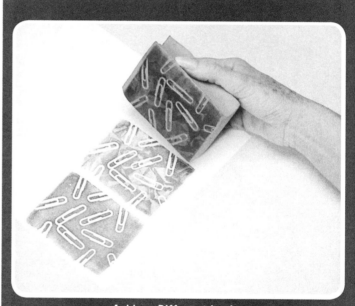

Achieve Different Looks

11 Raffia is a great background to experiment with.

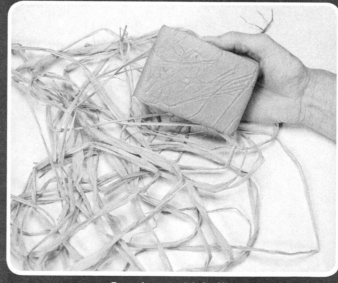

Experiment with Raffia

Experiment with Rainbow Inkpads

12Rainbow inkpads add interesting dimension too.

Texture Stamps and Hand-Dyed Papers

13Use texture stamps to add metallic inks to hand-dyed papers for an elegant finishing touch.

Create a Stamp: Method Two

Here is another fun way to create your own stamp.

Must-Haves: Materials

Tacky glue and white glue • Chipboard • One piece of twine • Scissors • Double-sided tape • Block of wood or acrylic • One piece of Penscore cut to the same size as the wood or acrylic block • Heat gun • One piece of felt • Plastic plate • Ink for stamping

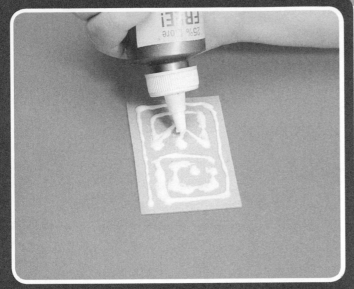

Apply White Glue to Chipboard

1 Use the white glue to draw a design on the chipboard. Work freehand, or draw a design and trace it with the glue.

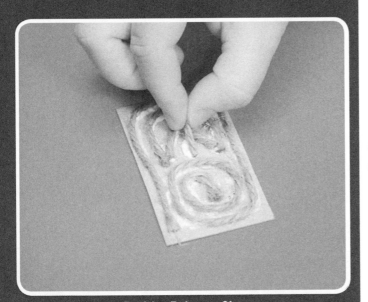

Position Twine on Glue

2 Cut pieces of twine and position them on the glue as shown.

Attach Chipboard to Block

3 Once the glue has dried, apply double-stick tape to attach the chipboard with the design on it to the block.

4 Heat the Penscore with the heat gun for a minute. Impress your image into it.

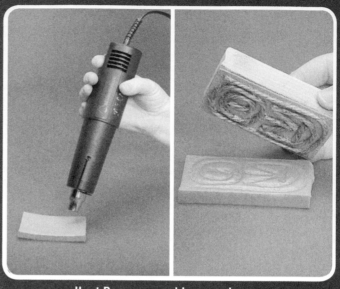

Heat Penscore and Impress Image

5 Attach the Penscore to the back of the block. You may want to use two pieces of wood to keep your hands cleaner while you stamp.

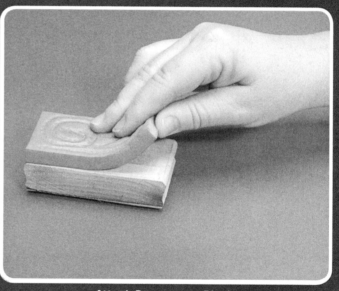

Attach Penscore to Block

6 Create a disposable rainbow inkpad by applying different colors in a striped pattern. Ink the stamp.

Create Rainbow Inkpad

Stamp in Alternating Blocks

7 Stamp in alternating blocks. Leave room for the image from the other side of your stamp.

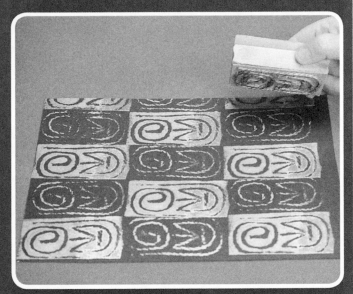

Ink Reverse Stamp and Fill in Gaps

8 Ink the reverse stamp and fill in the gaps to create a desired design on your paper.

Design Your Own Paper

Beautiful paper is an important aspect of stamping. Receiving a hand-made card is a joy in an age of commercially produced sentiments. Here you'll learn how to transform computer paper and dye-based inks into inexpensive designer paper for backgrounds, wrapping paper, and stamping surfaces.

Must-Haves: Materials

Butterscotch and Pitch Black Adirondack ink pads • Computer paper • Spray bottle filled with water • Paper towels • Heat tool

1 Carefully remove lid of first inkpad. Rub it over the entire paper surface.

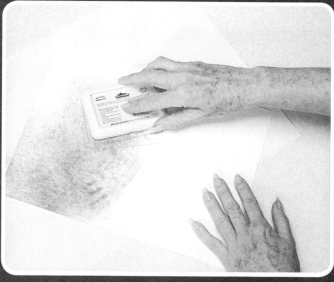

Rub Ink

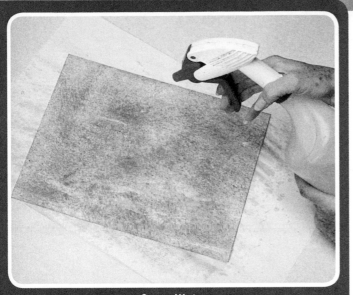

Spray Water

2 Spray paper with water until the ink bleeds together.

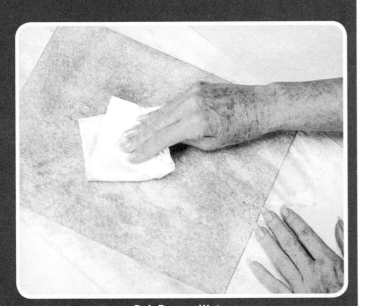

Dab Excess Water

3 Dab off any excess water with paper towels.

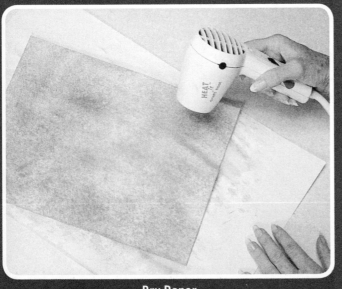

Dry Paper

4 Dry paper with a heat tool.

5 Crumple paper to create texture. Carefully unfold paper and lay flat.

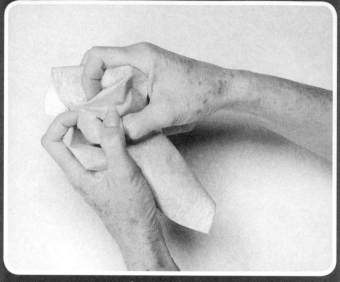

Crumple Paper

6 Remove lid from second ink pad. Rub it firmly over the textured areas.

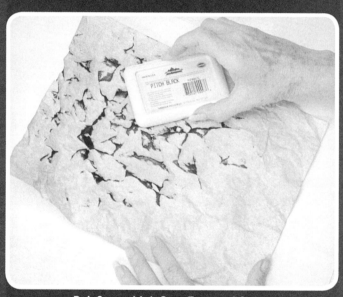

Rub Second Ink Over Textured Areas

7 Spray with water.

Spray Water

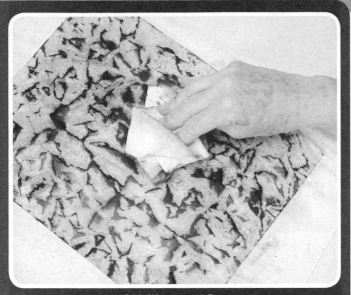

Dab Water and Dry

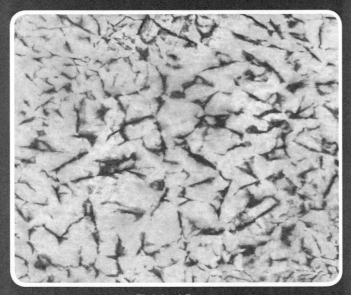

Finished Paper

Finished Paper Used as Wrapping Paper

8 Dab any excess water with paper towels. Heat-dry or air-dry if time permits.

Create an Envelope Without a Template

There is a template in this book (on page 41) that you can use to make envelopes. There are also templates you can purchase at craft stores if you prefer. Or, you can try this method, which requires no template at all.

Must-Haves: Materials

Finished card to measure for sizing the envelope • 8½" x 11" paper • Scissors • Double-stick tape or glue

1 Lay the card on the paper so that you can fold up from the bottom and still have an ample flap for the closure. Crease paper well.

Fold Paper and Adjust for Closure

Fold Top Flap

2 Fold the top flap down. Crease well.

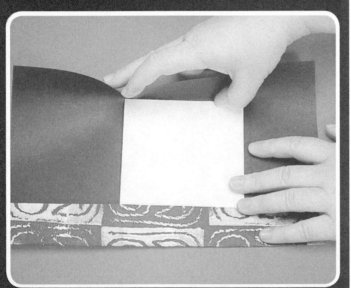

Fold Sides In

3 Open the paper out and fold the insides in, still following the card configuration and crease well.

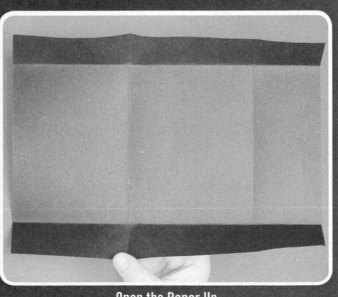

Open the Paper Up

4 Open the paper out flat so that you can see all the creases.

Continues

5 Snip the corners out of the paper at a slight angle.

Snip Corners

6 Apply double-stick tape or glue to the edges.

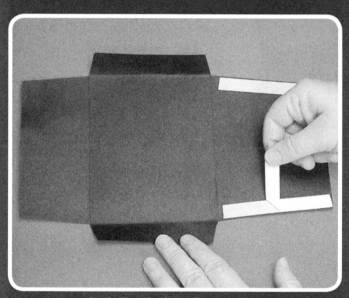

Apply Double-Stick Tape or Glue

7 Press firmly to seal edges.

Seal Edges

Before You Begin

Remember you're reading this book to learn how to create beautiful, handmade projects. Each craft is something that takes work, energy, and effort. The first rule is that you want to have fun and you're reading to turn that energy into gorgeous artwork. Don't be scared if you're unsure about a technique or step. Look at the visuals closely. Your finished piece does not have to look exactly or remotely like what is in this book. It's all in what you want and what you desire. It's your imagination, so don't forget to use it!

Elements of the Book

Don't forget that there are little advice pieces sprinkled throughout the instructions. They're called "*Tips & Quips*" and they're more likely than not important to read and follow. You'll also notice that Part III is called Extra Credit Fun. These projects are included for those who feel they're ready for more of a challenge, but they are also included because a beginner *can* complete them with a little effort.

 It's time to go get crafty!

Part II

Projects 101

Personal Portfolio

Attractive and practical, this unique kit is handy for holding important documents and other items. Try covering it with fabric for an especially unique look. The dimensions given for this project will allow the folio to contain 8½" × 11" papers nicely.

 Must-Haves: Materials

12" × 26" chipboard • Patterns below • Knife for scoring • Stylus • Black book tape or photographic blackout tape (optional trim) • YES! Glue • One sheet of black 8½" × 11" cardstock • Clips • One sheet of 8½" × 11" black text-weight paper • Straightedge • Decorative paper • Magnetic strips • Something to decorate the front flap

Tape Flap Back On

1 Transfer the first pattern to the long piece of chipboard. Score one side of the board with a knife. Score the other side with a stylus. Fold the board towards the stylus score. Cut off the flap portion and use paper tape to tape it back on, leaving a gap of about ⅛". You only need to tape one side.

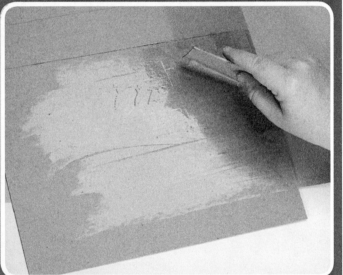

Spread YES! Glue onto Folio

2 Use a chipboard scrap to spread the YES! glue onto one section of the folio at a time.

Smooth and Crease Decorative Paper

3 Smooth the decorative paper over the first chipboard section and then spread an even coat of glue onto the next section. Cover the chipboard by gluing and smoothing one section at a time and using the edge of the table to make each crease as you work.

Continues

4 Creasing the paper is crucial to keep the cover paper from tearing as you fold the folio into place.

Crease the Paper

5 Flip the body over and cut darts into the cover paper at each fold point.

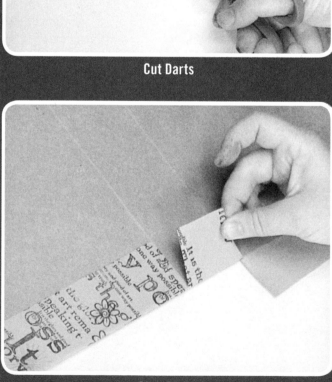

Cut Darts

6 Glue all the edges into place.

Glue Edges

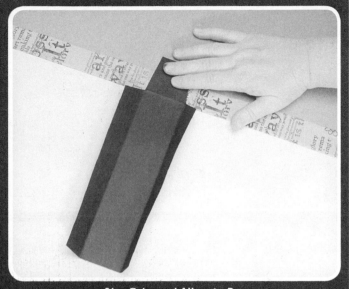

Glue Tabs and Allow to Dry

7 Cut the 8½" × 11" cardstock in half lengthwise. Use the pattern above to cut side gussets. Glue the tabs into place at the bottom fold. Allow to dry completely before you move on to the next step.

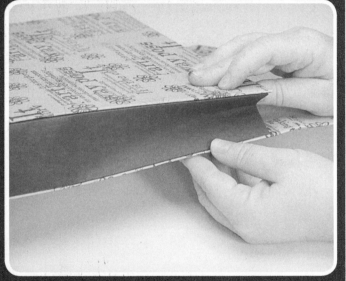

Pinch Top of Gusset Together

8 After the bottom flap is dry on the side gusset, glue the side tabs into place just inside the edge of the chipboard body. Pinch the top of the gusset together and use clips to hold the edges while they are drying. Remember to use scrap chipboard placed between the clips and the body to keep the clips from marring your project surface.

Cut out Front Flap

9 Trace the front flap onto a piece of 8½" × 11" text-weight paper. Cut this out and use as a liner.

Continues

29

10 Glue the liner into place. Use a stylus and a straight-edge to make sure that the liner paper is glued down and creased nicely at the folds.

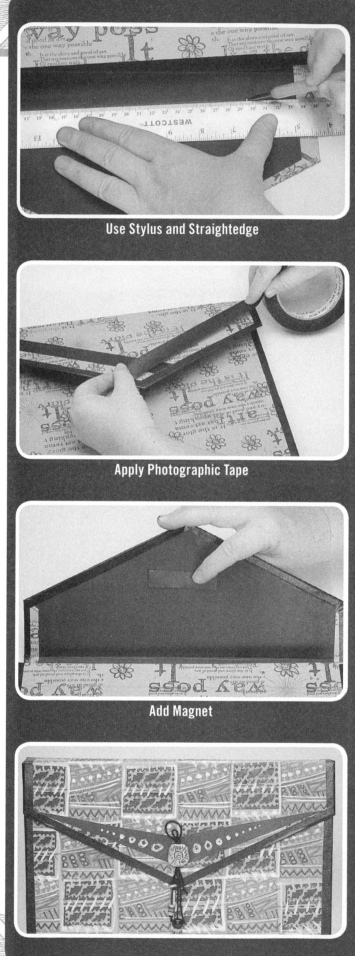

Use Stylus and Straightedge

11 Use photographic tape to apply an attractive black edge to the entire folio and a crisscross design on the front flap—this is optional.

Apply Photographic Tape

12 Attach a decoration to the front flap and a magnet for the closure.

Add Magnet

Tips & Quips: Stamping on kraft paper and then drawing over the whole design with a gold Krylon marker results in this decorative paper cover. Note the use of beads for embellishment.

The Perfect Pin

EnviroTex Lite can be used to make pins, necklaces, bracelets, charms, and medallions for your books and boxes. There are lots and lots of uses for this particular project so go ahead, have fun, and know that you are producing a valuable and lovely piece of artwork.

 Must-Haves: Materials

Stamps • Embossing ink and gold embossing powder • Black paper • Heat gun • Colored pencils, including white • Chipboard • Glue stick • Push pins and a piece of foamcore • Poster tack putty • Craft stick or stirring tool • EnviroTex Lite or any brand of resin • Plastic measuring cup • Utility knife • Black felt-tip pen • Black backing cardstock (or leather, or felt) • Pinback • Glue stick and tacky glue

1 Stamp an image in embossing ink on black paper and emboss (using the heat gun) with gold embossing powder. Use a sharp white colored pencil to color a base coat. Try to avoid running into the embossing with your pencil because it could nick off the embossing powder. After you've penciled your white base coat, color over it as desired. The white undercoat will make the colored pencil show up much better on the black paper.

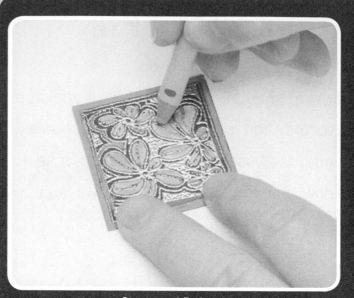

Stamp and Emboss

2 Glue the colored image onto the piece of chipboard with a glue stick.

Glue Image onto Chipboard

3 Coat the edges with embossing ink.

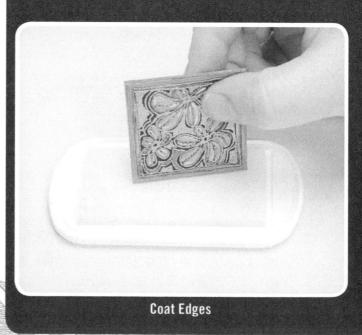

Coat Edges

Dip Edges into Embossing Powder

4 Pour a small amount of gold embossing powder onto a scrap piece of paper and dip the edges of the pin into it.

Emboss Edges

5 Emboss the edges, making sure not to aim the gun at your fingers.

Here are two pins on their stands ready for the Envi-roTex. Note that the projects are on raised pins so that you can use a craft stick to wipe off drips that may form under the project.

Place Project onto Poster Tack

6 Stick the push pin into the foamcore and place a small amount of poster tack putty on top of the pin. Place the project piece onto the poster tack securely. Larger pieces will require three tacks to stand evenly.

Continues

7 Pour a small amount of resin (try to mix only what you will use) into a mixing cup and then add an equal amount of catalyst. Mix well for about two minutes. If you do not mix equal parts resin and catalyst, or you don't mix them well, you will have a mess that dries sticky to the touch.

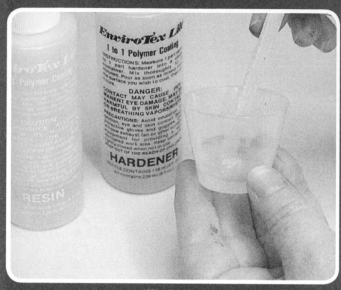

Mix Resin

8 Use the craft stick to coat the edge of the project with resin. Pour a small amount of resin on top of the project and use the stick to smooth it out. Don't worry about the air bubbles—they will work their way out in a couple of minutes. If there are stubborn bubbles, blow gently to pop them.

Coat with Resin

9 After the resin has dried overnight, use a utility knife to carefully dig just beneath the surface of the chipboard to remove any drips. Don't try to cut through the resin with your knife.

Use Utility Knife to Remove Drips

Use Felt-Tip Pen

10 Use a felt-tip pen to color the back edges of the chipboard.

Measure for the Opening

11 Cut a piece of black backing cardstock (leather and felt work great as backings, too) and lay the pinback down to measure for the opening.

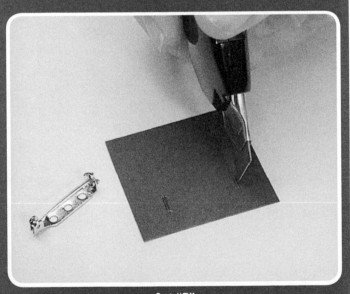

Cut "T"

12 Cut a tiny "T" shape so that you can insert the ends of the pinback into the liner as shown.

Continues

13 Use tack glue to coat the back side of the liner.

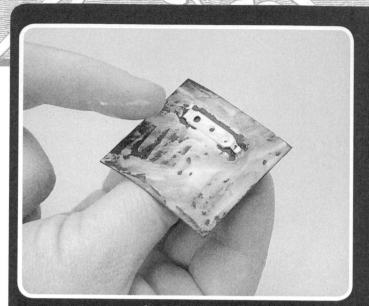

Apply Tack Glue

14 Place the liner and pinback on the back of your project and press down to secure them.

Secure Liner and Pinback on Project

Handy Light

This lamp has a metallic finish called Chemtek, which is great for a new or aged look. Environmentally friendly, this lamp makes an ideal house-warming gift!

⭐ **Must-Haves: Materials**

Four-sided lamp • Brush • Chemtek: steel, rust • Copper metal sheeting • Hand stamp • Permanent ink, black • Pergamano tool • Spray adhesive • Sandpaper

1 With a brush, coat the lamp with steel Chemtek.

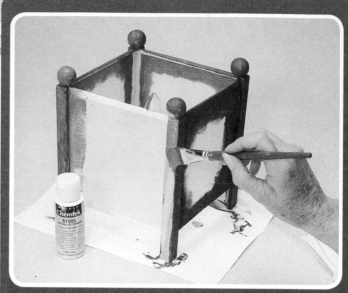

Coat Lamp

2 Cut out four equal-sized squares of copper metal sheeting. Stamp images on them with permanent black ink.

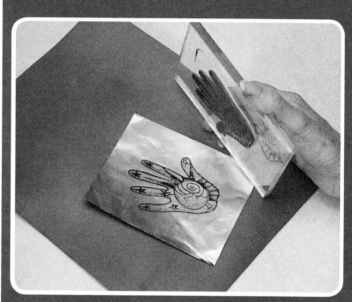

Stamp Squares

3 Sponge on rust Chemtek.

Sponge Chemtek

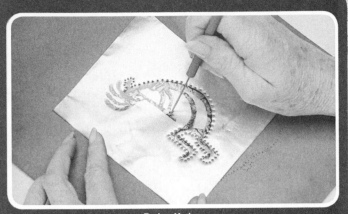

Poke Holes

Coat with Spray Adhesive

Secure Pieces to Lamp

Sand Edges

4 With a pergamano tool, poke holes around the image so that when the lamp is turned on, the light will shine through.

5 Coat the finished metal pieces with spray adhesive.

6 Secure metal pieces to the now-rusted lamp.

7 Sand the rough edges.

Fancy Folio

What better way to organize your stationery or small belongings than in a pretty and practical folio? This little kit is terrific for housing many other gifts—do you want to give a set of photos, a CD, or another small gift to a friend? As with all the projects in this book, this pattern is easy to tailor to any desired size and you can make the kit as simple or as embellished as you wish.

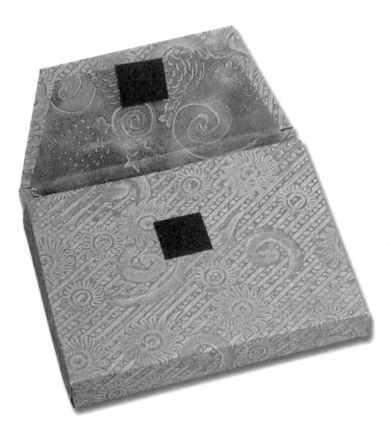

 Must-Haves: Materials

Thin piece of chipboard or posterboard cut to the pattern provided on page 41 • Knife • Stylus • Permanent spray adhesive • Sheet of decorative paper large enough to cover the chipboard or posterboard • Smaller decorative papers • Double-stick tape • Stationery cards and envelopes • Paper for liner • 3M Super 77 spray adhesive • Clear nail polish (optional for the paper medallion on the front of your folio, should you use one) • Self-stick hook-and-loop tape or magnetic tape for the closure

2

5/8

4½

½

4½

½ | 5¾ | ½

Pattern

Tips & Quips: Copy this pattern onto heavy-weight cardstock or construction paper. Posterboard is also a good material to use. Cut the box out on the solid lines. Glue the paste paper down to the board and smooth well. Trim paper up to edges of the board. Use stamps to decorate the inside of the box. Score with stylus on the inside and fold the box on the dotted lines. Use tacky glue to glue tabs together. Use self-stick magnets for a closure (optional). Decorate the flap of the box and stationery cards with pieces of chipboard, Dimensional Magic, and paste paper scraps.

Continues

1 Cut out and score the body of the folio on both sides. Remember that to make nice edges on the folds in chipboard, you must score with a knife on the outside and score with a stylus on the inside of the fold. Then, if you've scored deeply enough with the knife, it should be easy to make a clean fold. Cover the board evenly and entirely with permanent spray adhesive.

Spray Board with Permanent Spray Adhesive

2 Place the glued board onto the backside of the decorative paper cover and smooth it out. Use your knife to cut right up to the edges.

Use Knife to Cut

3 Glue the side paper tabs to the chipboard tabs. Use a strip of double-stick tape for this part, but glue works just as well.

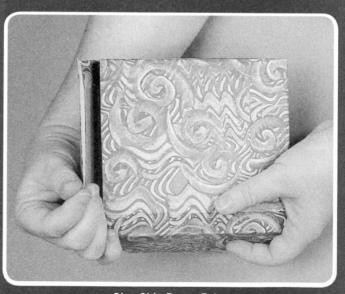

Glue Side Paper Tabs

Adhere Liner into Place

Bend the Front Flap Down

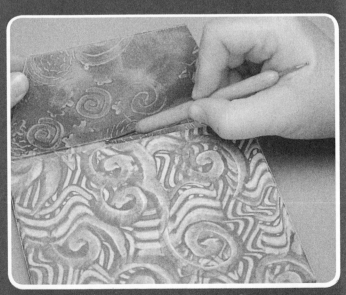

Use the Stylus to Enhance the Crease

4 Use spray mount or glue to adhere the liner into place.

Tips & Quips: When you cut out the decorative paper, refer to the pattern on page 41 to be sure to cut out an edge on each side of the paper. This is not really shown in the photographs, so make sure you don't forget. These side paper tabs will be folded over and glued to the chipboard side tabs.

5 After the liner is positioned, carefully bend the front flap down, molding the liner into the crease.

6 Use a stylus to further define the crease.

Continues

7 Stick one side of the magnet (or hook-and-loop tape) in place on the flap and lay the second side in place, bringing the self-stick magnet down to its corresponding position on the front of the folio.

Stick Magnet in Place

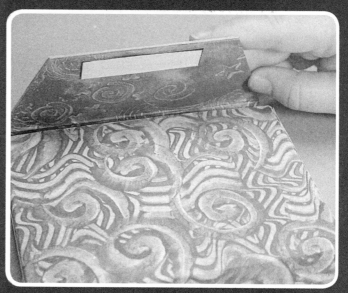

Secure Magnet

8 Decorate the front of the folio and the note cards as desired.

Decorate Folio as Desired

I'll Give You My Heart Box

Use your imagination and experiment with other stamps and types of shrink wrap to create a box for every occasion!

Must-Haves: Materials

Heart-shaped papier-mâché box • Shrink plastic, white • Pen or pencil • Scissors • Almost Leather sheet (optional) • Moon stamp • Permanent ink, black • Heat tool • Makeup sponge • Stream Adirondack ink pad • Penscore foam block (optional) • Pigment ink pad • Suze Weinberg's Ultra Thick Embossing Bronze Enamel • Tiny stones or beads

1 Use the heart box lid as a template to draw a heart on the shrink plastic.

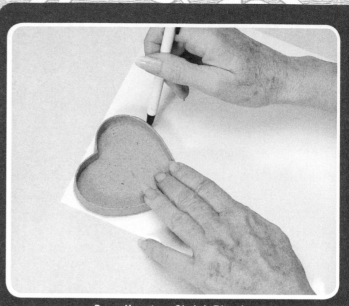

Draw Heart on Shrink Plastic

2 Cut out the shrink plastic heart with scissors.

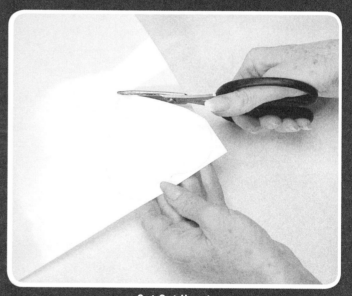

Cut Out Heart

3 Lay the heart on the Almost Leather sheet (it makes a great stamping cushion). Stamp a design using permanent black ink.

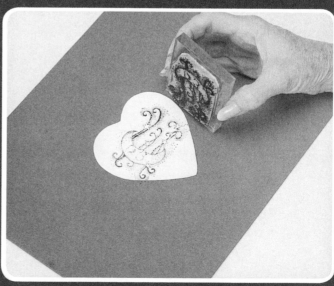

Stamp Design

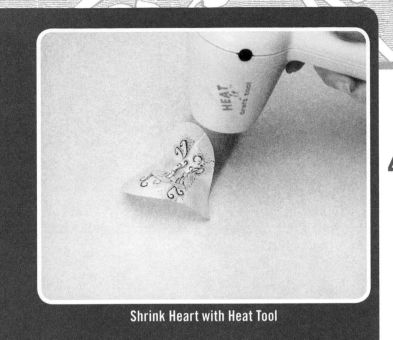

Shrink Heart with Heat Tool

4 Shrink the heart with a heat tool.

Stop Applying Heat When Piece Lies Flat

5 You'll know when the piece is done when it lies flat.

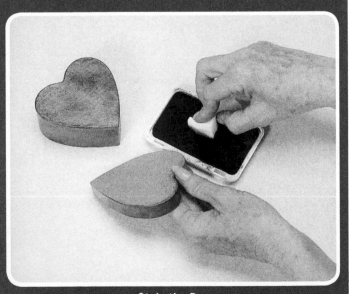

Stain the Box

6 Stain the box with your favorite ink using a makeup sponge.

7 If desired, add more ink with Penscore to give a textured look. (To learn how to use Penscore to add texture, see page 7.)

Add More Penscore If Desired

8 Using a pigment ink pad, dab ink all over the box lid.

Dab Ink on Box Lid

9 Saturate the entire lid with embossing powder.

Apply Embossing Powder to Lid

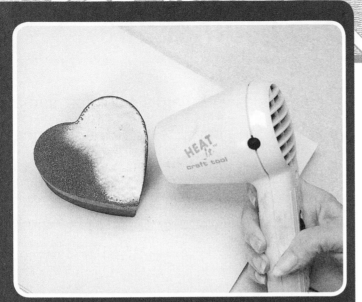

Use Heat Tool and Add More Powder

10 Melt the powder with a heat tool, and while still hot, add another layer of powder.

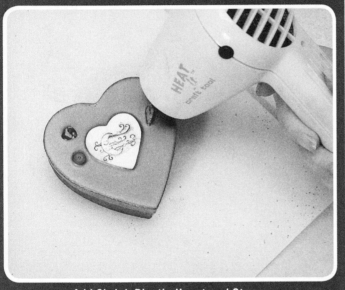

Add Shrink Plastic Heart and Stones

11 While the embossing powder is still hot, drop a shrink plastic heart on the lid. Keep heating, and drop stones randomly. Set aside to cool.

Light Up My Life Lampshade

You can make extraordinary lampshades with hardly any effort and a whole lot of imagination! To get started simply tear off the covering of an old lampshade to expose a plain white heatproof shade—an excellent base for stamped papers!

 Must-Haves: Materials

Lampshade • Dye ink pads, including a black waterproof ink pad • Paper to stamp on (60 lb white drawing paper was used for this particular project) • Scissors • Gold Krylon leafing pen • Stamp • Glue stick and tacky glue • Finishing tape (cloth tape works too) • Tacky glue • Fancy trim (optional)

Create Pattern

1 The easiest way to create a pattern for your lampshade is to color the edges, top and bottom, with a dye ink pad.

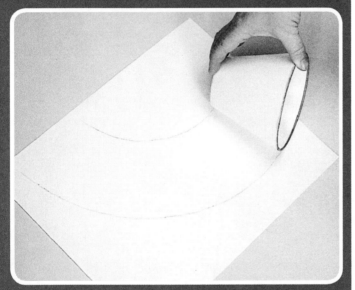

Roll Lampshade Across Paper

2 Start at one edge of your paper and roll the lampshade very carefully across the paper, depositing an inked line for a guide. If you want to make a self-edging, cut the paper a little larger than the pattern on both top and bottom. Add only a ⅜" margin, which should be sufficient to turn the stamped paper under and cover the metal frame.

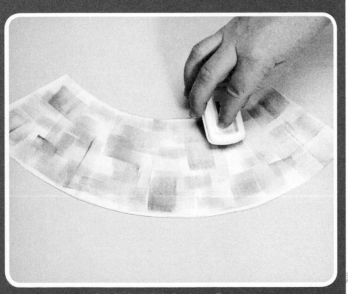

Apply Dye Ink Pads to Paper

3 Use the dye ink pads to apply the ink colors directly on the paper by touching down and dragging them in alternate directions. The mini Vivid! ink pads from Clearsnap are perfect for this.

Continues

4 Add a little shine using the gold marker.

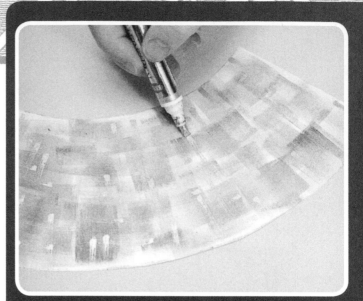
Add Shine

5 Use another stamp to apply a second color.

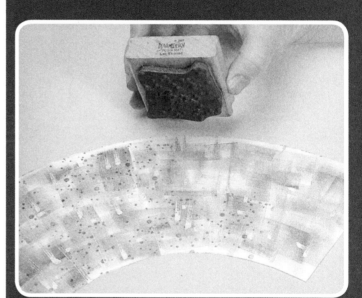
Apply Second Color

6 Stamp random images in black ink.

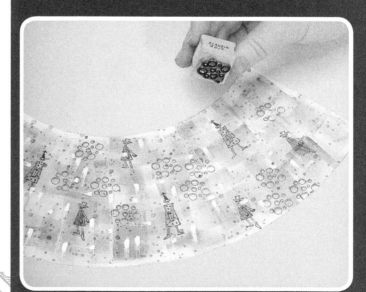
Stamp Random Images

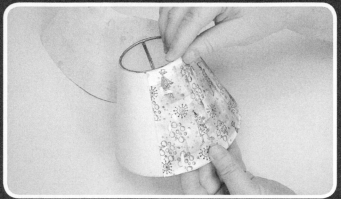

Apply Paper to Lampshade

7 Use a glue stick to apply the paper to the lampshade. Remember, with glue sticks, you must get good and total coverage. Too little glue will make the project pop apart. Position the stamped paper on the shade and smooth it down.

Apply Black Tape

8 Use the black tape as a finish (optional). Again, ribbons and fabric work well, and so does cutting the paper leaving a ⅜" margin and folding it in for a self-finish.

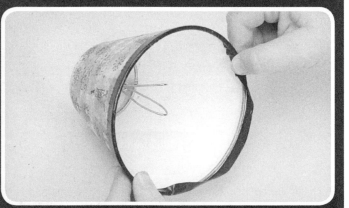

Snip Tape and Fold, Smoothing Out Wrinkles

9 Snip little cuts into the tape and fold it inward, smoothing out the overlaps and any crinkles you may make. Trim the inside tape with a knife, if necessary.

Position Trim with Tacky Glue

10 Use tacky glue to fix the trim into place.

Continues

Here's a shade where the decorative paper is colored brushed with markers scribbled over white tissue paper. The tissue was adhered to the white art paper and spritzed with water so the color would bleed onto the white paper. Then a random pattern of stamps was created.

This sophisticated shade was prepared with black stamping over white paper. The gold-leafed swirls were easy, too. Just squirt a little leafing adhesive (found in craft stores) into a plastic dish. Spread it out to an even layer and ink your stamp with the adhesive. Stamp onto the shade paper, and allow to dry. Remember to wash the adhesive off your stamp before it dries. After the adhesive dries to a tacky finish, apply gold leaf by laying it on the adhesive and brushing off any excess leaf.

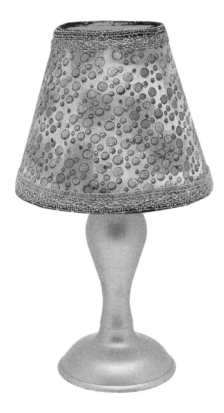

This shade was created with the same ink pad dragging method as in the Light Up My Life Lampshade project. The bubbles were stamped in black permanent ink and colored with markers.

Paperback Protector

Do you enjoy buying books for yourself and for friends and family? If so, try making a handy cover to shield those paperback novels.

 Must-Haves: Materials

2 Almost Leather sheets: brown, black • Heat tool • Penscore foam block • Anything with texture (basket, raffia, shoe) • Décor-it inks: mahogany, verdigris, gold • Scrap paper • Deckle scissors • Permanent ink, black • Makeup sponges • Kokopelli stamp • Small stone • Pen • Craft knife • Spray adhesive • Jewel Bond glue • 24" black cord • Bead to secure cord

1 Using the heat tool, completely heat both sides of the brown Almost Leather sheet until it shrinks evenly and looks smooth and leathery.

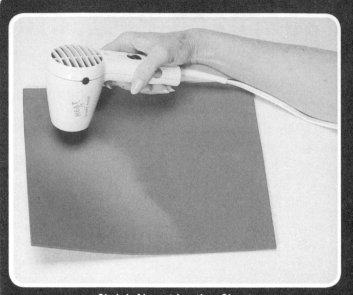

Shrink Almost Leather Sheet

2 Create a texture stamp with foam. (See the Create a Stamp technique on page 7.)

3 Squeeze your first selection of ink onto scrap paper. Ink the foam and randomly stamp on the leather piece to add texture.

Stamp on Almost Leather

4 Repeat with a second color of ink.

Stamp Using Second Color

Fold Book Cover and Heat

5 Fold the book cover in half, holding tightly while heating the edge with the heat tool.

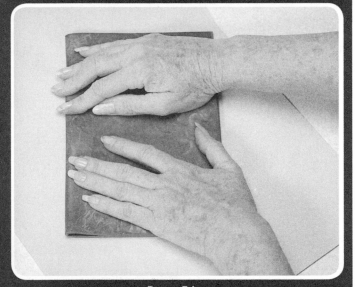

Press Edge

6 Press the edge down while cooling; the book cover should stay closed.

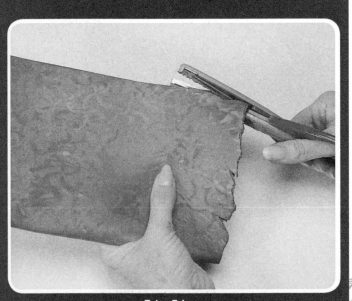

Trim Edges

7 While holding the cover firmly, slightly trim the edges with deckle scissors.

Continues ▶ **57**

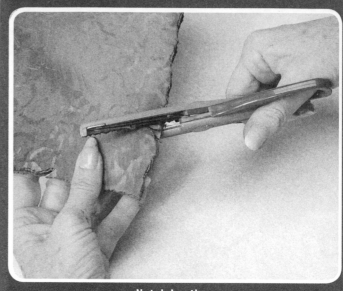

Notch Leather

8 Randomly notch the leather to give it a torn look.

Sponge Edges

9 Squeeze out a small amount of black permanent ink onto scrap paper. Sponge onto the edges of the cover to give it an aged look.

Stamp Black Almost Leather

10 Cut a 4½" × 4½" piece of black Almost Leather using deckle scissors. Heat both sides until soft, then stamp.

Personal Portfolio

PAGE 50

Light Up My Life Lampshade

PAGE 129

Fantastic Fabric Accessory

PAGE 40

Fancy Folio

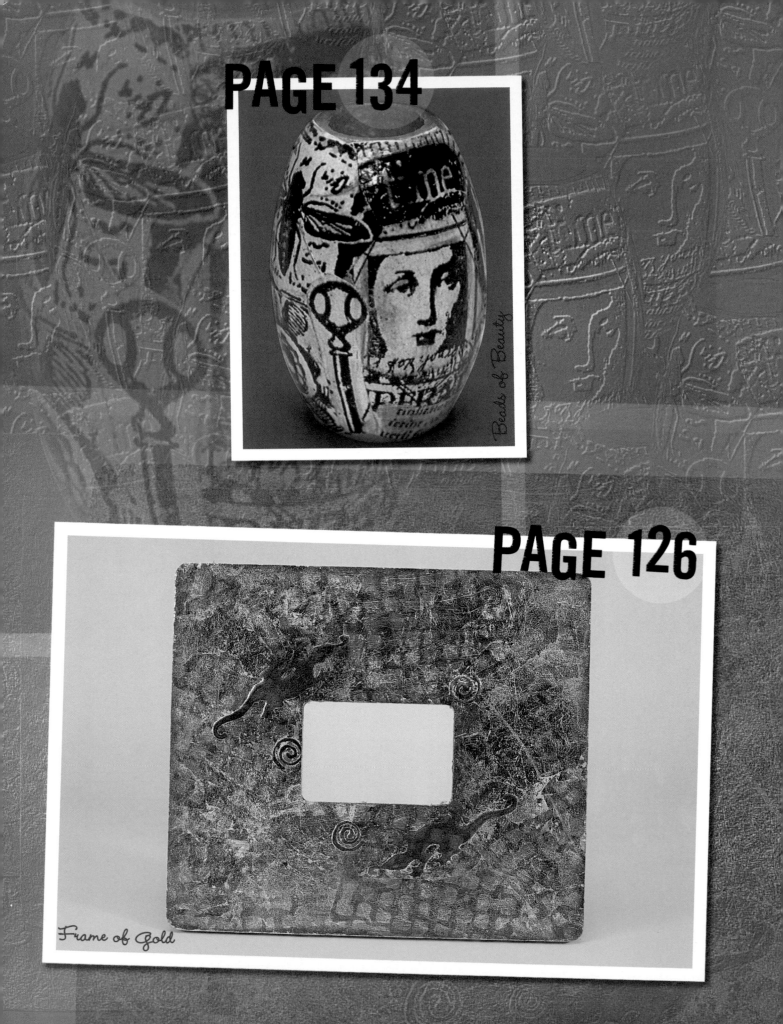

PAGE 134

Beads of Beauty

PAGE 126

Frame of Gold

PAGE 140

Fancy Fabric Note Cover

PAGE 103

DECORATIVE

A handcrafted item by Sandra McCall

Precious Push-Pins

PAGE 61

Tiny Tassle Book

PAGE 92

Idea Box

PAGE 75

Tiny Treasure Box

Key to My Art

PAGE 78

Add Turquoise Stone

11 Add a turquoise stone on the lower right part of the image and trace around it with a pen.

Cut a Hole

12 Cut a hole with a craft knife so the stone will embed itself into it.

Sponge Ink

13 Lightly sponge your second ink around the stamp area. Repeat with your third ink color.

14 Spray adhesive onto the back of the black piece and let it dry for ten minutes. Press it onto the upper portion of the book cover. Glue the stone in place.

Glue Stone

15 Fold the cord in half and place it half inside, half outside the cover. Pull the ends together tightly and knot.

16 Feed a bead onto the cords, pull up to knot, and knot again.

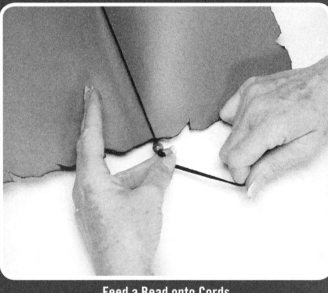

Feed a Bead onto Cords

Tiny Tassel Book

Perfect for jotting little notes to yourself, this tiny blank book also makes a great homemade gift. Decorate the tags with art or writing and try using metallic tape for a border instead of embossed tape.

 Must-Haves: Materials

Eight shipping tags • One piece of styrene or other plastic • One piece of colored cardstock • One piece of chipboard for the back cover • Plastic-cutting knife • Paper punch • Drill with ¼" bit • Doily • Watercolors and paintbrush • Heart stamp • Text stamp • Waterproof ink and a brush • Colored pencils • Dye ink pads • Stipple brush • Glue stick • Sailor Rolling Ball Glue Pen • Metal transfer foil • Embossable double-stick tape (Wonder or Miracle Tape, not Scotch) • Scissors • Gold embossing powder • Scratch paper • Heating tool • Tapestry needle • One yard each of four or five different fancy fibers • Two-holed plain button • One fancy button • Fray Check

1 Use a utility knife and a straightedge to cut a piece of chipboard slightly larger than the shipping tags. A ¼" margin on three sides is best. Make the top edge flush with the tags.

Cut Chipboard

2 Cut one piece of cardstock and one piece of plastic exactly the same size as the chipboard back. Use styrene so that you can use a pair of old scissors to cut it. Scissors may chip acrylic and Plexiglas, so you will need to use a plastic-cutting knife for them. You can use a paper punch to punch the holes out of the chipboard and the paper, but you'll have to use a drill for creating a hole in the plastic. Use a regular hand drill with a ¼" drill bit.

Cut Cardstock and Plastic

3 To start this collage, color a doily with watercolor washes.

Color Doily

Stamp Images with Waterproof Ink

4 Stamp your images in waterproof ink and color them with watercolors and/or colored pencils. Don't be afraid to paint over the lines! Use colored pencils to add detail if desired.

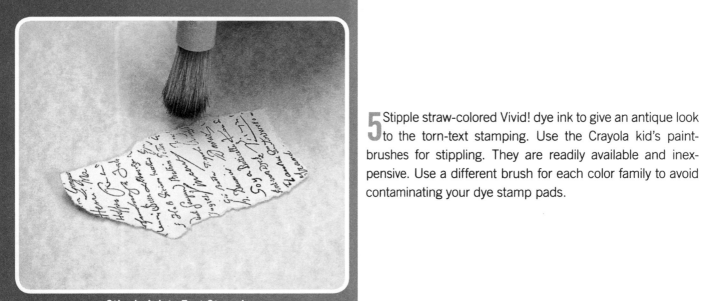

Stipple Ink to Text Stamping

5 Stipple straw-colored Vivid! dye ink to give an antique look to the torn-text stamping. Use the Crayola kid's paint-brushes for stippling. They are readily available and inexpensive. Use a different brush for each color family to avoid contaminating your dye stamp pads.

Start Applying Layers

Tips & Quips: **Styrene comes with a blue protective film on both sides. Simply peel this off of each side before assembly.**

6 To assemble your collage, use a glue stick and start applying the layers to the background cardstock.

Continues

7 Add the doily and stamped, colored cutouts to your collage.

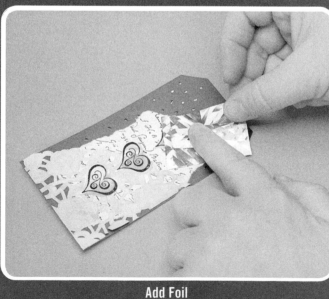

Add Doily and Cutouts

8 Use the Sailor Rolling Ball Glue Pen to apply small dots of glue to the places where you want to apply the foil. This glue is blue when it comes out of the tube and dries completely clear. This is a two-way glue so that when the coat is dry, it will still be tacky.

Use Glue Pen

9 Place the foil, dull side down, onto the completely dry dots of glue. Rub the foil to make good contact with the glue and peel up the foil paper.

Add Foil

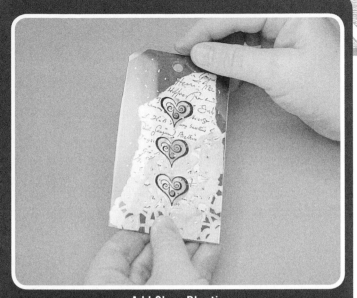

Add Clear Plastic

10 Run a fine line of glue stick onto the edges of your collage and place the clear plastic on top.

Add Double-Stick Tape

11 Run a length of double-stick tape around the edges of the sandwiched front cover.

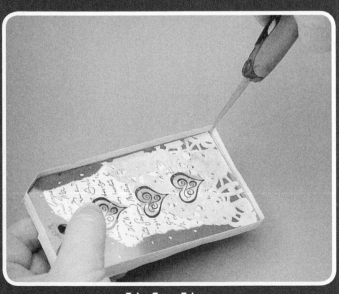

Trim Tape Edges

12 Trim the corner edges of the tape on the front and the back of the cover.

Continues

13 Fold one edge of the tape over the cover and press down firmly. (If you don't press the edges down very well, embossing powder may get under them and prevent the tape from sticking to the cover.) Peel off the paper backing one edge at a time so that you don't trap your paper under the previous edge's tape. You can miter the corners if you wish.

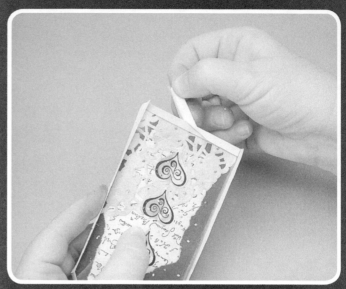

Peel Off Paper Backing

14 Pour the embossing powder onto a sheet of scratch paper and lay the taped edges over it to pick up the powder. Press well to get the powder to stick all over the tape. Use a soft paintbrush to brush off any excess powder. Heat each edge and then wave the piece around in the air gently to cool it off. Continuous heat may cause the plastic to warp. Remember not to aim the gun at your fingers. If the plastic gets too hot for you to handle, hold it with a pair of pliers during embossing.

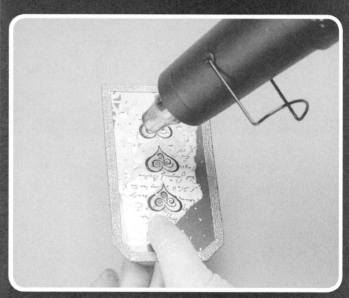

Pour Embossing Powder

15 To assemble the book, thread a needle with a length of matching fiber and run it through one side of the back button, up through the chipboard, the tags, the cover, and the fancy button; then back down through the stack.

Run Thread Through Back Button, Chipboard, Tags, Cover, and Fancy Button

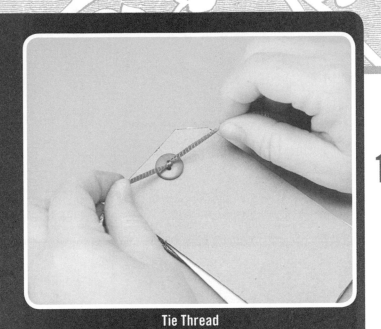

Tie Thread

16 Tie off the back thread with a knot.

Secure Knot

17 Use Fray Check to secure the knot firmly and trim the ends off leaving ½".

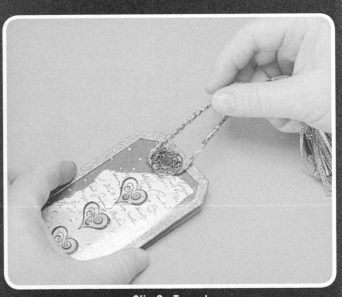

Slip On Tassel

18 Slip the braided hang tassel (see instructions below) under the fancy button on the front cover. The pressure of the tied button will hold the tassel in place.

Completed Project

Tassel Assembly

The following instructions and visuals show the tie of the cord at the top of the tassel. For this book, position the knot so that it will be buried in the bulb of the tassel above the wrapped neck.

1 Wrap fibers around a piece of chipboard. Wrap as many times as you like, which will determine how full your tassel will be.

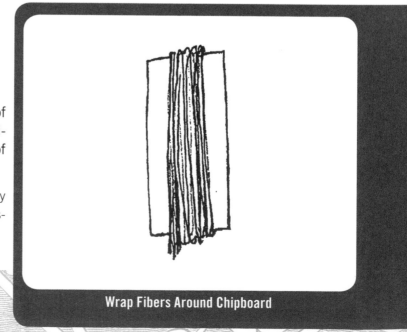

Wrap Fibers Around Chipboard

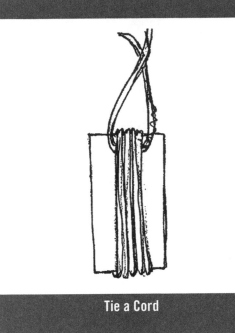

Tie a Cord

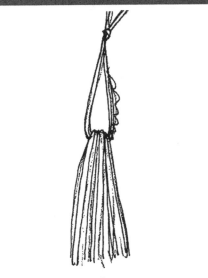

Slip Fibers off Chipboard

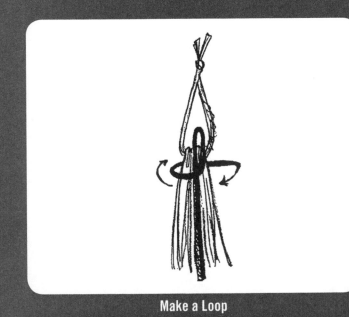

Make a Loop

2 Tie a cord around and under the tassel.

3 Slip the fibers off the chipboard and cut them at the ends.

4 Hold a length of fiber next to the tassel as shown, making a loop at the top and leaving a little tail. Note the color of the tail. You will have to find the tail again in a minute.

Continues ➤

Wrap Fiber Around Loop

5 Wrap the fiber around the loop, catching it securely, and continue to wrap up toward the loop.

6 Slip the tail of the wrapped cord into the loop, find the original tail, and give a little tug downward. Pull the original loop and the final tail into the wrapped neck of the tassel to hide the ends.

Candle Décor

Take any plain candle lying around—or purchase some at a discount store and transform them into beautiful, decorative works of art by using the stamping and embossing techniques explained on these next few pages.

 Must-Haves: Materials

White or pastel candle • Unryu paper, white • Scissors • Stamps of your choice • Permanent ink, black • Bright rainbow ink pad • Cotton swabs • Heat tool • Dark-colored candle • Paper towels • Décor-it ink, copper • Scrap paper • Makeup sponges • Embellishments such as yarn and beads (optional)

Stamping

1 Cut the paper to fit around the white candle and make sure the paper is ¼" shorter than the candle's height.

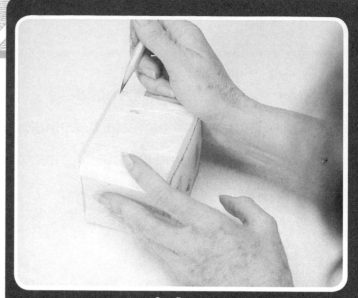

Cut Paper

2 Stamp designs using black permanent ink.

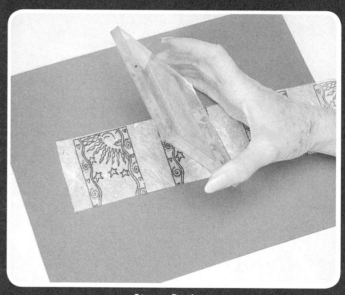

Stamp Designs

3 Color the designs with a rainbow ink pad using cotton swabs.

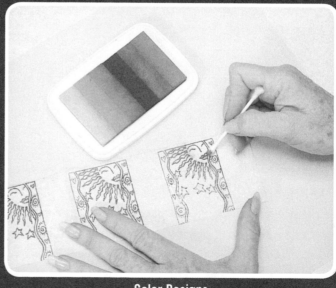

Color Designs

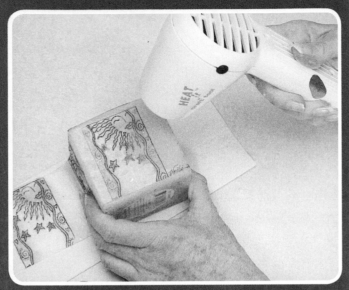

Melt Paper onto Candle

4 Lay the stamped paper on top of the candle and hold it tight while heating the wax with the heat tool. The paper will melt onto the candle. Continue to heat and press paper into the wax all the way around the candle.

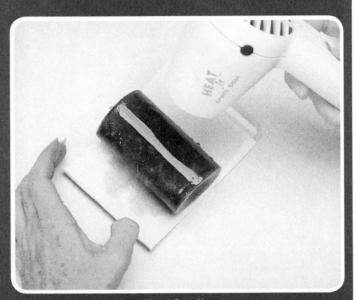

Heat Candle

Embossing

1 Lay the dark-colored candle on a folded paper towel to keep it from rocking. Heat the candle surface area to be stamped until it appears wet.

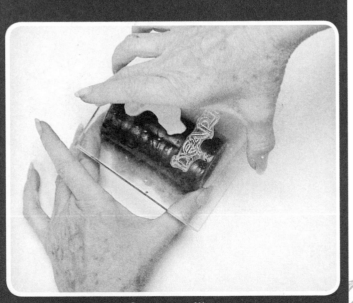

Stamp onto Wax

2 Let the candle cool for a minute until the candle clouds over. Quickly stamp onto the melted wax.

Continues

3 Hold the stamp in the wax for a few seconds, then carefully rock the stamp until it easily releases from the candle.

Rock Stamp

4 Squeeze a little ink of your choice on scrap paper. Using a makeup sponge, lightly rub ink across the stamped areas of the candle to create contrast. Add yarns and beads for decoration.

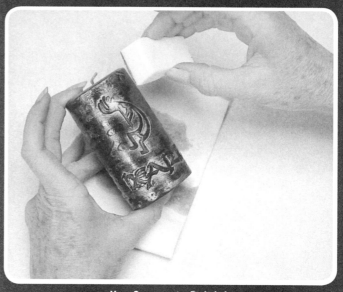

Use Sponge to Rub Ink

Tiny Treasure Box

With a few simple tools, you can create an extraordinary treasure box. There are few things as beautiful and as breathtaking as the effects of burning tin. Don't create just one, create at least two so you can present one as a gift to a friend!

 ### Must-Haves: Materials

Tin container (An inexpensive brass-coated pillbox was used for this project. If you find such a box that says it's from China, chances are it's made of tin with a very thin coat of brass that will burn off in the fire. That is the type of box you want.) • Tongs or needle-nose pliers • Clear embossing ink pad • Ultra Thick Embossing Enamel or Amazing Glaze • Stamps with bold images • Colored embossing powders • Silver Rub 'n Buff and Metallic Rub-ons

1 With tongs or needle-nose pliers, hold the tin box in a flame until the coating burns off and the swirls of iridescent color emerge. Remember to douse the hot tin in cold water before you touch it.

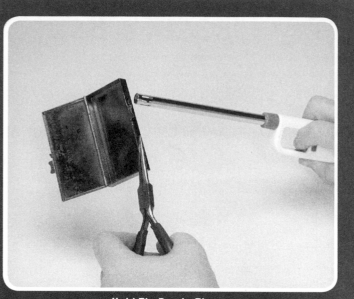

Hold Tin Box in Flame

2 Apply the clear embossing ink all over the top of the container.

Apply Clear Embossing Ink

3 Emboss the top with a coat of Ultra Thick Embossing Enamel or Amazing Glaze. While still hot, pour a second coat on the box top and heat to melt. Repeat for a third coat and while the powder is still hot, sprinkle other colors and heat to melt.

Sprinkle Other Colors and Heat

Stamp and Hold

4 While the embossing powder is hot, press the stamp into it and hold it for several seconds until the powder cools.

This tin has been finished with clear powder and topped with silver Rub 'n Buff and Metallic Rub-ons. You can use a cloth to apply these products, but your fingers will give you better control over the application. The coloring products are oil-based and will take a day to cure. You may need to seal them with Krylon Crystal Clear if you want to use the box immediately.

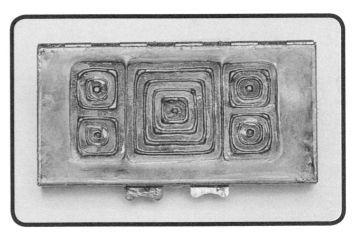

Key to My Art

These miniature boxes are so simple to make, and are also great as pins, amulets, or decorations for your home or office. Don't let that stop you from making this cute project into something else such as a gift or creative piece of jewelry!

Must-Haves: Materials

Two pieces of chipboard cut to 2¼" × 3" • One piece of tooling metal cut to about 2¾" × 3½" • Utility Cutter • Styrene cut to 2¼" × 3" • Stylus • Markers for writing on slick surfaces • Paper towels • Assorted trinkets for collage • Tweezers • Quick Grab glue or tacky glue • Stamped images • Stipple brush and dye ink pads • Black ¼" foamcore cut to 2¼" × 3" with a frame opening cut out so that the frame edge is just a little smaller than ¼" • Black felt tip pen

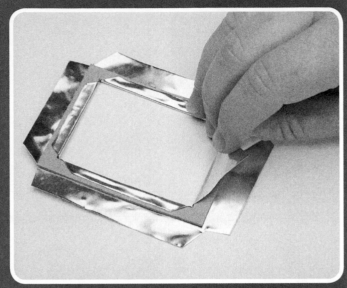

Trim and Fold Up Inside Edges

Sandwich Styrene

Use Stylus

1 Measure and cut out the center of one of the pieces of chipboard to make a frame that is ¼" wide on all sides. Center the frame on the piece of metal. Using a utility cutter, cut an "X" in the center from corner to corner of the inside chipboard frame piece. Trim and fold up the inside edges to the backside of the frame piece.

2 Sandwich the styrene next to the frame piece and fold the metal edges up and over it to hold the plastic securely in place.

3 Use a stylus or any pointed tool to inscribe designs on the front of the metal frame. You want your creation to have the charm of a handcrafted item, so don't worry about imperfection of lines or tracing a pattern.

Continues

4 Use a marker and a paper towel to brush on and rub off color until satisfied.

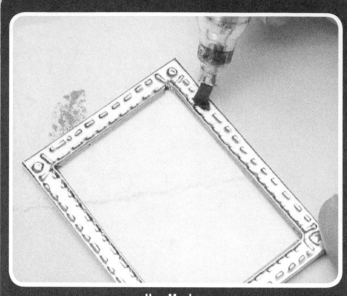

Use Marker

5 To achieve the same look as in the photo, use a gold Marvy metallic marker after the previous layer of orange Design marker.

Use a Marvy Metallic Marker

6 Collect trinkets for your project—don't worry about the strange or brassy colors. You can use markers or paints to color them later.

Collect Trinkets

Assemble Collage

7 Assemble the collage on top of the uncut piece of chipboard for your back piece. It's a good idea to glue a piece of paste paper to the chipboard before you apply the collage elements to it. Use a glue stick for the paper elements and Quick Grab or tacky glue for the charms and leaves. Color your stamped images with a stipple brush and dye ink pads.

Glue Foamcore Frame onto Collaged Piece

8 Glue the foamcore frame onto the collaged piece of chipboard backing and then use Quick Grab or tacky glue to attach the metal front assembly to the foamcore frame. Use a black felt tip pen to color the edges of the backing chipboard to match the black foamcore.

This is a slightly more complicated piece that was made by cutting a piece of foamcore in the approximate shape of an angel and then gluing metal findings and tooled metal cuttings onto it. See the ornate top and bottom section? That's the plastic ornament cut in half. The whole assembly was "aged" with Instant Rust products. The framed shadow box was glued to the center of the assembly.

Metal Décor

This is a fun way to give copper sheeting an antique look. Get creative and experiment with different textures using stamps you created and other Fabrico ink colors.

Must-Haves: Materials

Copper metal quilting sheet • Almost Leather sheet • Permanent ink, black • Hand stamp • Deckle edge scissors • Brayer • Double-ball stylus • Wooden spindle • Makeup sponges • Fabrico inks: peony purple, burgundy • Heat tool • Double-sided foam tape

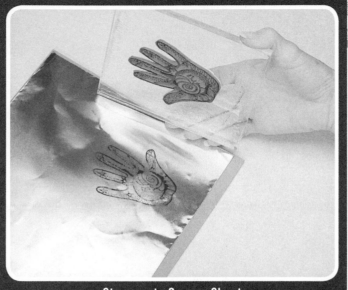

Stamp onto Copper Sheet

1 Place the metal quilting sheet on Almost Leather as a work surface. Using permanent black ink, stamp your design onto the copper sheet.

Wrinkle Metal Piece

2 Cut around the design with deckle scissors to create a square. Carefully wrinkle up the metal piece.

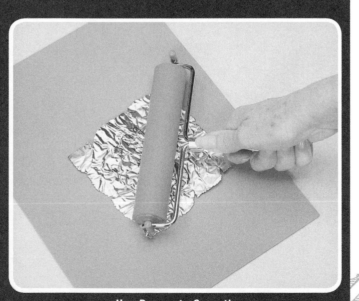

Use Brayer to Smooth

3 Lay the metal on top of the Almost Leather sheet. Using a brayer, smooth out the sheet.

Continues

4 Draw around the design with a stylus to create a quilted look.

5 Turn the piece over and lay it down on the Almost Leather sheet. Rub the inside of the design with the wooden spindle to puff out the image.

6 Using makeup sponges, lightly apply one ink randomly. Set it with a heat tool.

Use Stylus

Use Wooden Spindle

Randomly Apply Ink

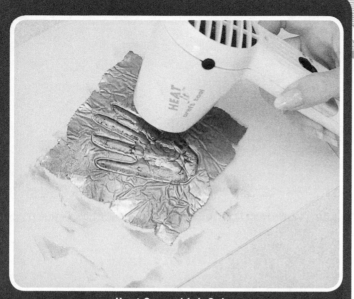

Heat Second Ink Color

7 Dab on a second ink color and heat it again.

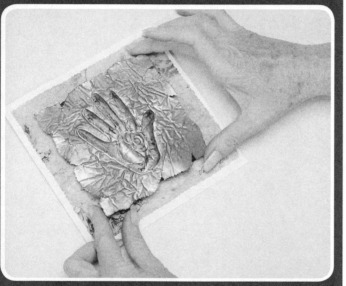

Apply Double-Sided Foam Tape

8 Cut pieces of double-sided foam tape. Apply it to the back of the metal.

Part III

Extra Credit Fun

Marvelous Memories Book

This album is excellent for the times when you need a fast gift that can be for anyone, young or old, male or female. The chipboard can be covered with decorative paper or left natural as shown. The overall design can easily be shifted with just a small change in the colors and materials used.

Must-Haves: Materials

One piece of chipboard • One piece of chipboard cut to the size of the front spine • One piece of rubber cut the same size as the back piece of chipboard • Text-weight paper for pages • Two-hole paper punch • Two screw posts, ½" in length or as desired • Two screws, same size as posts • Quick Grab glue • One medallion for the front cover

Hole-Punch for Screw Posts

1 Use the two-hole paper punch to create the holes for the screw posts. Insert the posts facing up from the back cover.

Lay Papers onto Posts

2 Lay your punched stack of text-weight papers onto the posts as shown.

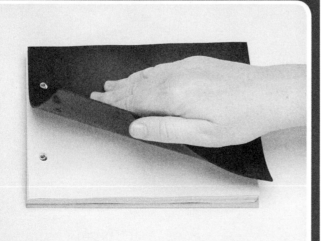

Lay Rubber Sheet on Top

3 Lay the punched rubber sheet on top of the text block.

4 Lay the spine piece on top of the rubber.

Lay Spine Piece on Top

5 Place the screws into position and tighten them. A screw-driver may help in tightening the screws, but the screws should twist into the posts with minimal effort.

Place Screws into Position

6 Use the Quick Grab glue to set the medallion in place.

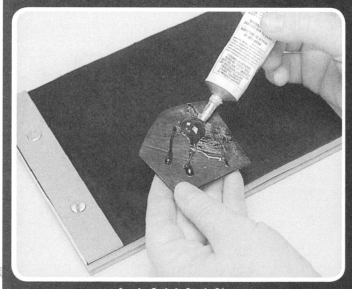

Apply Quick Grab Glue

PAGE 115

PAGE 71

Candle Décor 1

PAGE 71

Candle Décor 2

Handy Light

PAGE 88

Marvelous Memories Book

PAGE 31

The Perfect Pin

PAGE 100

Vesta 2000

Classy Clay Charm

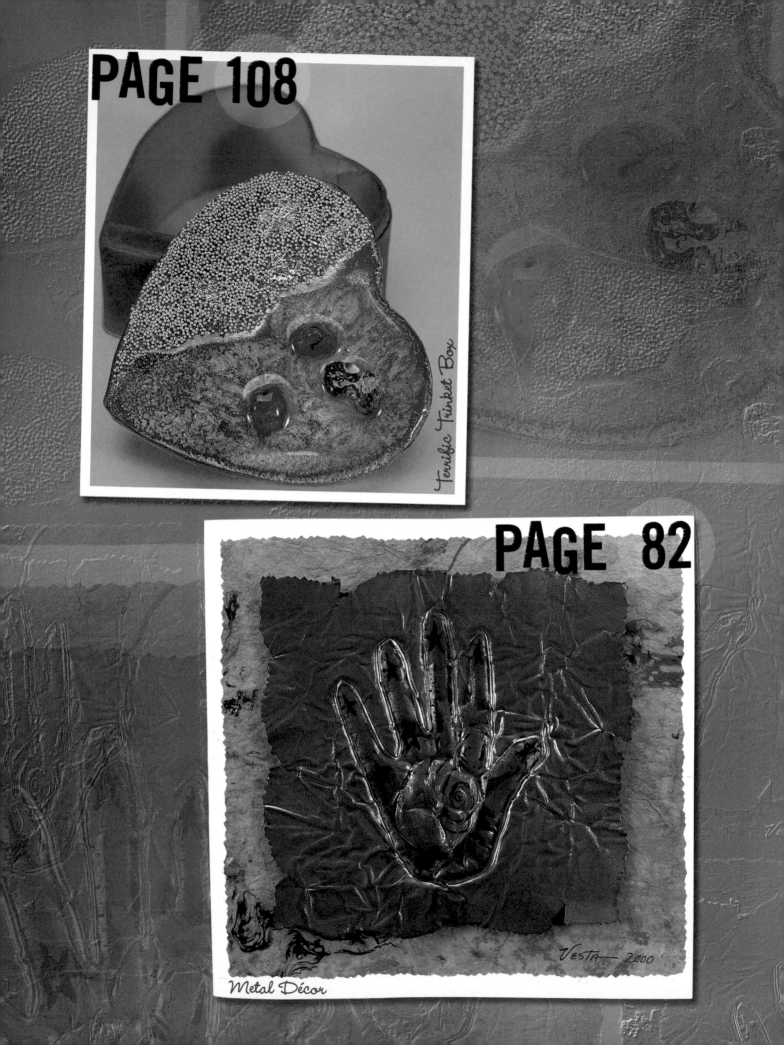

PAGE 108

Terrific Trinket Box

PAGE 82

Metal Décor

PAGE 45

I'll Give You My Heart Box

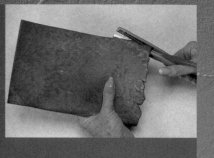

PAGE 55

Paperback Protector

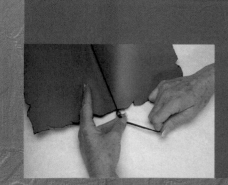

Press Firmly

7 Press medallion firmly into place.

Tips & Quips: The album shown here has a paper-clay medallion layered over a piece of burned copper, then a piece of screen. Quick Grab glue is great for holding these different items together.

Idea Box

Allow your personality to shine through with this crafty kit. Made up of random embellishments and decoration, a smaller version of this project makes a great pin!

Must-Haves: Materials

Pattern below • Piece of thick chipboard • Stylus • Knife • Tape • Glue • Paper for back of box • Paper to line the interior (optional) • UHU glue stick or YES! Glue • White acrylic paint • Stamps • Ink pads • Stipple brush • Piece of styrene or plastic • Decorative paper • Decorations for each "window" of the box

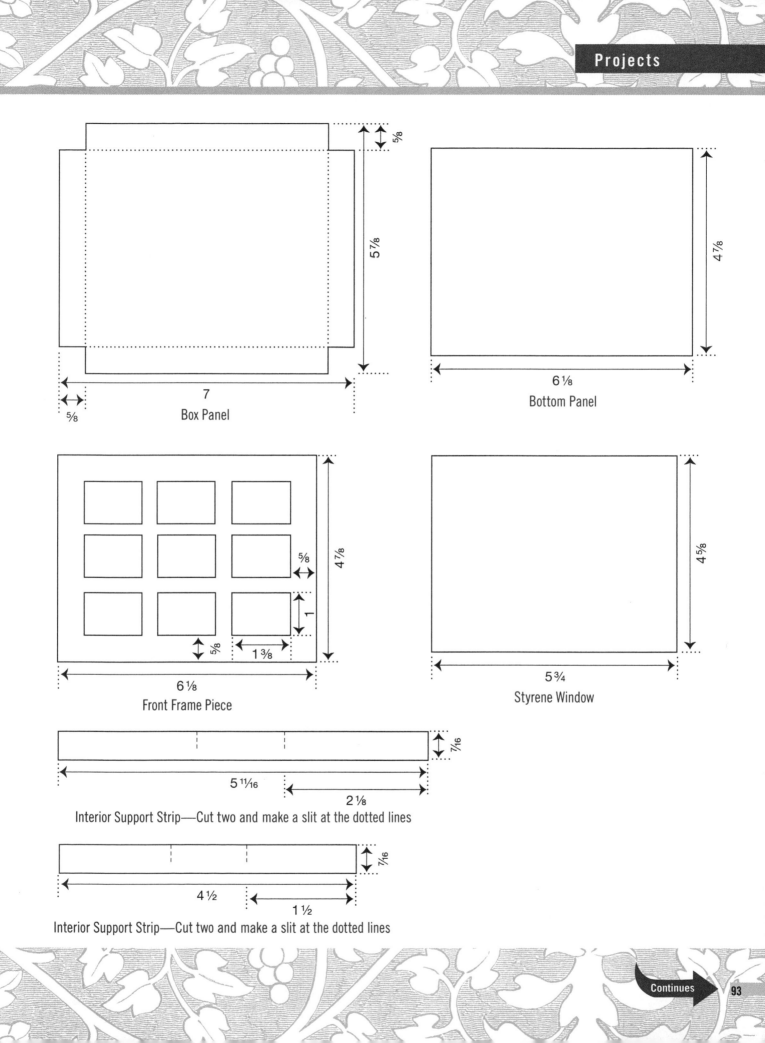

5/8

5 7/8

7

5/8

Box Panel

4 7/8

6 1/8

Bottom Panel

5/8

4 7/8

1

5/8

1 3/8

6 1/8

Front Frame Piece

4 5/8

5 3/4

Styrene Window

7/16

5 11/16

2 1/8

Interior Support Strip—Cut two and make a slit at the dotted lines

7/16

4 1/2

1 1/2

Interior Support Strip—Cut two and make a slit at the dotted lines

1 Transfer the measurements of the shadow box pattern to the chipboard. Cut out all the pieces: one top panel with the windows cut out, one bottom panel, one inner box piece, two short sides, two long sides, two short cross pieces, and two long cross pieces.

2 Use a stylus to score one side of the inner box piece, then flip it over and use a knife to score the other side along the dotted lines. Fold the sides up with the knife score on the outside edge.

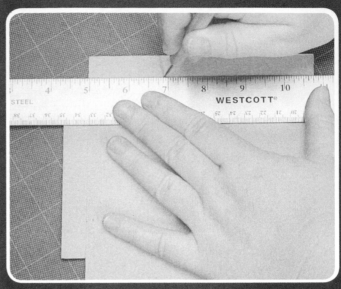

Use Knife to Score Along Dotted Lines

3 Use tape to secure the corners on the box piece.

Apply Tape

4 Remember that the folded outside edge is the part that has been scored with the knife.

Scored Edge

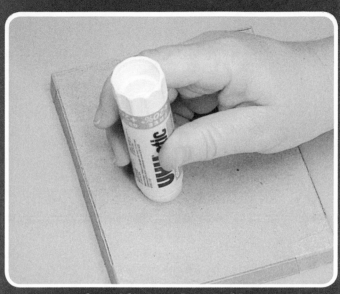

Spread Glue over Bottom of Box

5 Spread glue over the bottom of the box and cover it with paper.

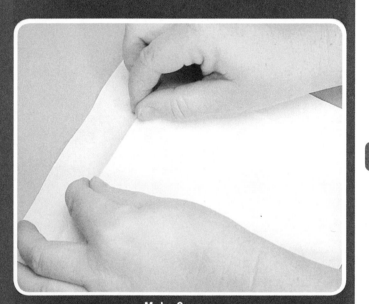

Make Crease

6 Make a crease along the edges as shown.

Clip Darts

7 Clip darts out of the corners of the paper as shown, leaving tabs on the long edges.

Continues

8 Glue the long, tabbed edges in first, then glue the endpapers into place to cover the box.

Glue Long, Tabbed Edges, Then Glue Endpapers

9 Cut a piece of paper to line the inside bottom of the box. This is optional.

Line Inside of Box

10 Cover the bottom panel with paper.

Cover Bottom Panel

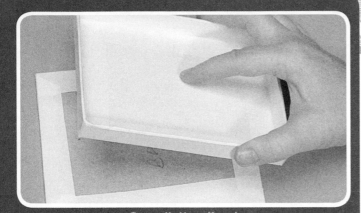

Cover Bottom Panel

11 Glue bottom panel paper to the backside of the box assembly. Use tacky or YES! glue.

Apply Tacky Glue

12 Paint the cross strips with white acrylic paint and allow them to dry. Assemble all four pieces by interlocking them together. Put tacky glue on the ends and place them down into the box section.

Allow Assembly to Dry

13 Hold pieces in place until glue starts to set. Allow the assembly to dry.

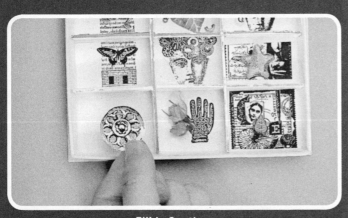

Fill in Sections

14 Stamp and color your images with the stipple brush. Fill the box sections with fun items.

Continues

15 Cut the styrene to fit into the box section, and use tacky glue to secure it to the crossed support assembly.

Cut Styrene

16 Cut the window frame following the pattern measurements.

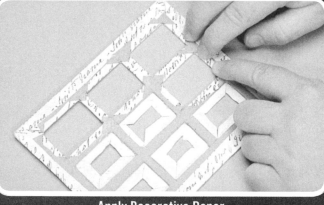

Cut Window Frame

17 Cover the frame with decorative paper.

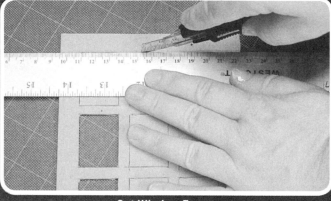

Apply Decorative Paper

18 Put tacky glue on the back of the frame and lay it over the top piece, holding it in place until the glue starts to set.

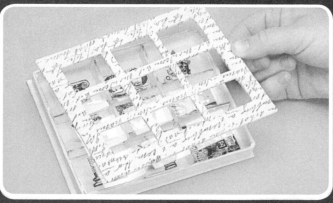

Adhere Back Frame with Top Piece

This particular box was created using a large text stamp and small seashells for the interior decoration. The decorative paper for the cover was created with marbling inks.

This version of the box has a frame that has an image stamped over white acrylic paint. Notice how the black ink was absorbed by the acrylic paint, turning the stamped image to a gray color.

Here is a miniversion of the box with only one "window." It makes an adorable pin.

Classy Clay Charm

Clay and stamping go hand in hand. Whether you're creating a mold or stamping directly into clay, this technique is easy for any beginner. Switch things up by playing with glitter and gold leaf.

 Must-Haves: Materials

Almost Leather sheet • Heat tool • Sun and moon face stamp • Polymer clay, black • Brayer • Décor-it metallic ink • Scrap paper • Makeup sponge

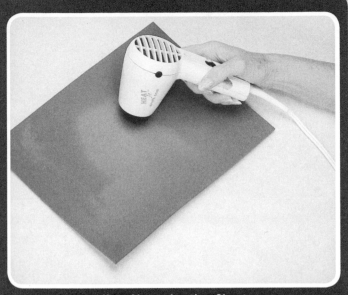

Heat Almost Leather Sheet

1 Heat the center area of the Almost Leather sheet until it is soft (a couple of minutes).

Stamp Design

2 Quickly and firmly stamp the design on softened foam.

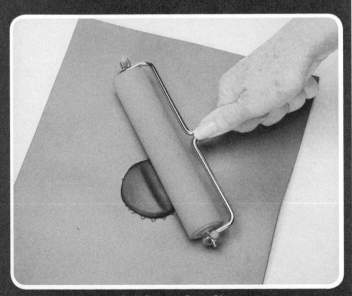

Roll Brayer Over Clay

3 Roll a small ball of black polymer clay until it is soft and smooth. Flatten and place over the "mold." Roll a brayer over the clay to force it down into the design.

Continues

4 Carefully peel up the design and bake according to the manufacturer's directions.

Bake Design

5 When the clay has cooled, squeeze a small amount of metallic ink on scrap paper. Using a makeup sponge, very lightly rub ink across the design to bring out the image.

Lightly Rub Ink

6 Use the clay as a charm, card embellishment, or for jewelry.

Add Clay for Card Embellishment

Precious Push-Pins

Shrink art is a unique technique you will learn by creating this project and hopefully, you'll take the technique to new levels by applying it to other crafts you make. Have fun!

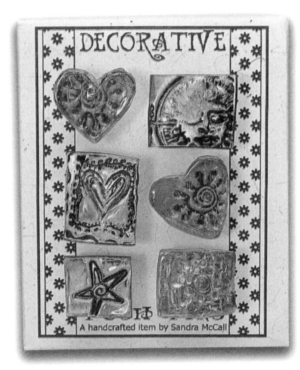

 Must-Haves: Materials

Black, clear, and opaque shrink plastic • Six push-pins • Heat tool • Stamps • Silver and colored Rub 'n Buff • Metallic Rub-ons • Glaze (Diamond Glaze, Dimensional Magic, or 3-D Crystal Lacquer) • Instant glue (such as QuickTite) • Ultrafine sandpaper • Permanent ink for nonporous surfaces in colors of your choice • Permanent ink cleaner to clean your stamps • Craft knife or awl • Plastic plate and felt for inkpad • Two pieces of ¼" foamcore cut to 2½" × 3½" or one piece of ½" thick foamcore cut to 2½" × 3½" • Decorative paper to cover the foamcore • Product labels (you can create them on your computer and print them out in sheets with four labels to a sheet) • Tacky glue • Clear plastic wrap

1 Cut out a shape freehand in black, clear, and opaque plastic. Remember to make it twice the size as you want the finished piece to be. Shrink it with your heat gun and impress a stamp into the hot plastic. Let the plastic cool for a little while before removing the stamp.

Shrink Shape with Heat Gun

2 Dab a little silver Rub 'n Buff onto the raised image.

Apply Silver Rub 'n Buff

3 Use Metallic Rub-ons to give the image color. Lightly dab this over the silver. While it's wet, it can accidentally be wiped right off very easily.

Apply Metallic Rub-ons

Coat with Glossy Finish

4 When the colors look the way you want them, coat the piece with one of the glossy finishes and let it dry. I use Diamond Glaze, 3-D Crystal Lacquer, or Dimensional Magic to get a shiny, raised, and rounded finish.

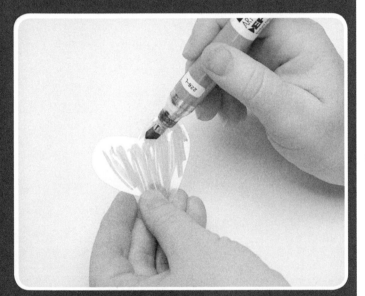

Cut Heart from Plastic

5 Cut a heart out of the clear plastic, sand lightly on both sides, and use permanent markers to color the back side.

Heat Heart and Stamp

6 Heat heart with the gun and stamp it with the stamp.

Continues

7 Put the silver and colored rub-ons on the raised part of the image, letting the attractive basecoat colors show through.

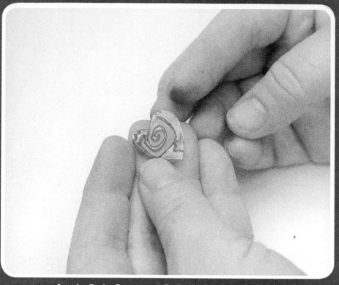

Apply Rub-Ons onto Raised Part of Image

8 Finish with Diamond Glaze.

Apply Glaze

9 Scratch both the push-pin and shrink art with your knife or an awl. Put a spot of instant glue on the pin and press both pieces together. Hold for about five seconds.

Adhere Pin to Piece

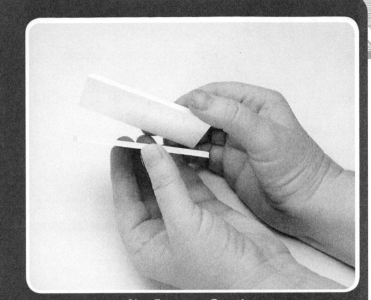

Glue Foamcore Together

Wrap Set Like a Present

10 To make the packaging, glue the two pieces of ¼" foamcore together (you can use ½" foamcore if you like) and then wrap it like it's a present. Sign the back of your set and glue the label on top.

11 Wrap your set in clear plastic wrap, and now you have finished!

Terrific Trinket Box

Use this box to store personal, sentimental, or random items for safekeeping in a lovely, decorative container.

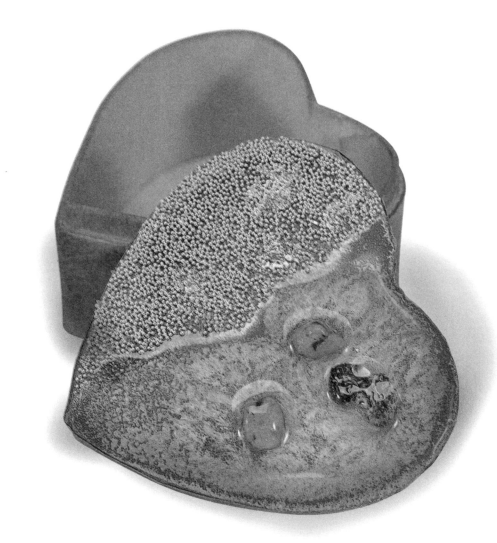

Must-Haves: Materials

Small heart-shaped papier-mâché box and lid • Eggplant Adirondack ink pad • Makeup sponges • Gold or Copper Décor-it ink • Spray acrylic topcoat • Ultimate bond tape • Pen or pencil • Scissors • Scrap paper • Cranberry and Eggplant Adirondack embossing powders • Heat tool • Embossing powder, clear • Several colorful stones • Gold leaf crumbs • Two colors of glass beads

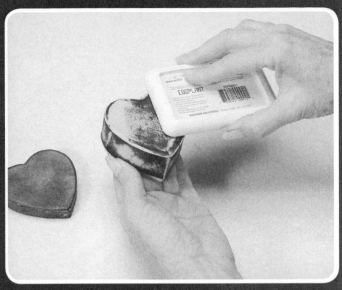

Rub Ink

1 Remove the lid from the ink pad. Rub it all over the heart box and lid.

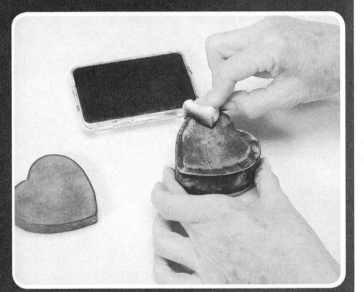

Add More Ink with Sponge

2 Blend and add more ink with a makeup sponge.

Sponge Gold or Copper Ink

3 Lightly sponge on gold or copper ink to give a burnished look.

Continues

4 Spray the entire box with acrylic coating.

Spray Box

5 Place the heart box lid on a sheet of tape and trace.

Trace Heart Lid

6 Cut out the tape heart and remove one side of the paper backing.

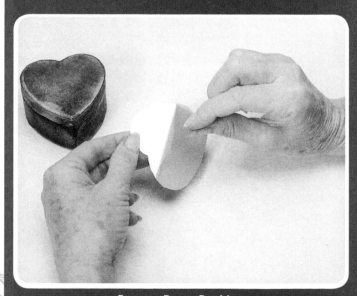

Remove Paper Backing

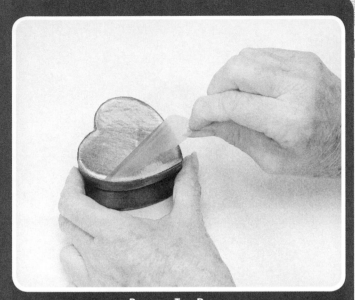

Remove Top Paper

7 Place the sticky heart tape on the box lid, rub to adhere, and remove the top paper.

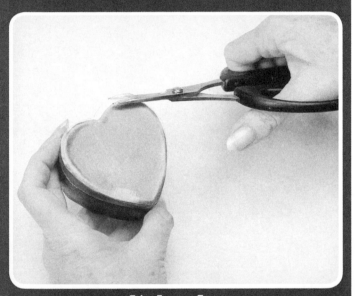

Trim Excess Tape

8 Trim any excess tape.

Apply First Color of Embossing Powder

9 Place the box lid on scrap paper and pour some of the first color of embossing powder on the right side of the sticky tape, shaking off any excess and returning it to the bottle.

Continues

10 Pour the second color of embossing powder over the first to give it a marbled look.

Apply Second Color of Embossing Powder

11 Heat with heat tool until melted.

Heat Until Melted

12 While the embossing powders are still hot, pour on clear embossing powder.

Pour Clear Embossing Powder

Heat Until Melted

13 Heat with heat tool until melted.

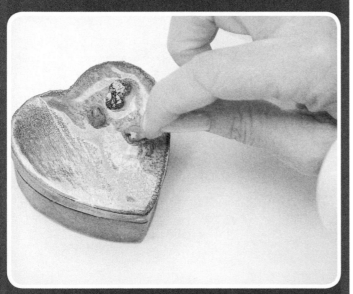

Add Stones

14 Drop colored stones onto the melted powder and let cool.

Disperse Gold Leaf

15 Wet your fingertips and pick up small amounts of gold leaf crumbs. Place them randomly on the left side of the box.

Continues

16 Hold the lid over a dish and pour some of the glass beads onto the sticky tape. Return any excess beads to the bottle.

Add Glass Beads

17 Pour a different color of glass beads over the remaining uncovered tape. Rub beads firmly to set.

Add Second Color of Glass Beads

Designer Display Kit

This attractive, easy-to-make box folds shut to resemble a book and can be as simple or as ornate as you like. With lots of room for stamp art in the process, this is a fun and easy little addition to just about anything you want to present or display.

 **Must-Haves: Materials**

Two equal size pieces of chipboard or mat board • Two pieces of ¼" thick foam-core cut to the appropriate size or one piece of ½" thick foamcore—remember that the foamcore should be ⅛" smaller than the covers so nothing peeks out • One piece of black text-weight paper large enough to cover your foamcore frame • Black cloth tape, such as book tape or black gaffer's tape • Scissors • Tacky glue, glue stick, and white glue • Decorative paper • Two pieces of black paper for liner, each cut to about 3¾" × 3¾" • ⅝" grosgrain ribbon for the book wrap • Fray Check • Black felt-tip pen • ⅝" D-ring • Self-stick hook-and-loop tape • One brass eyelet and a setting tool

1 Cut a piece of foamcore to desired size. Measure and mark the corners for a frame that is ½" wide.

Cut Foamcore to Desired Size

2 Cut out the frame. Use a straightedge to help you cut. With foamcore you need a very sharp blade to keep the foam from bunching up. Also, don't try to cut through the entire thickness in one swoop, especially if you're cutting thicker foamcore. Expect to make a cut through the first half and follow up with a second slice to break through the bottom sheet of paper.

Cut Frame

3 If using ¼" foamcore, use tacky glue to glue two pieces of foamcore together, making a frame that is ½" deep. Be sure to smooth out those lumps of glue for a nice bond.

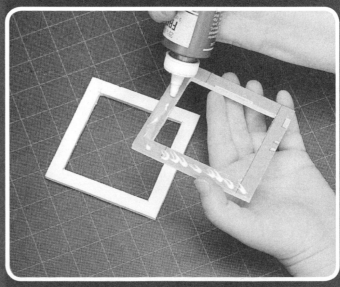

Apply Tacky Glue

Use Glue Stick

4 Use a glue stick to coat one side of the frame.

Cut "X"

5 Place the frame in the center of the black text-weight paper, turn it over and smooth out any wrinkles. Remember to use the heat of your hands to help speed up the drying time. Flip the assembly back over and cut an "X" on the black paper from corner to corner inside the frame.

Fold Triangle-Shaped Paper Up

6 Fold each triangle-shaped paper up and trim off the points so that the paper covers the back but doesn't peek out past the outside edge.

Continues

7 Cut little corner covers from a piece of the same black paper, fold them and apply white glue to adhere them firmly into place.

Tips & Quips: Gaffer's tape is found in photo or television studio supply houses. It is a coated fabric tape that has low tack, so when you lay it down lightly and it isn't positioned perfectly, you can peel it up easily without ripping your paper. After you press it down firmly, it stays in place. It is also nonreflective, which makes it perfect and pretty for this project.

8 Cut a little snip into the corner cover down to the frame corner. Use tacky glue to lay the corner pieces down on the backside of the frame.

9 Use tacky glue to glue the little triangle pieces up into place.

Create Corner Covers

Cut Into Corner Covers

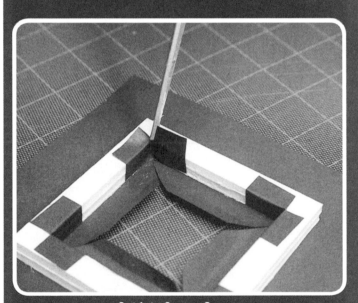

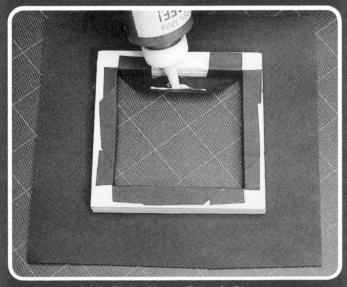

Apply Tacky Glue to Triangle Pieces

Cut Ends of Frame Cover

10 Cut the ends of the frame cover, making tabs as shown.

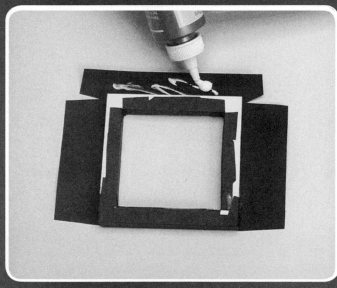

Apply Tacky Glue to Secure Tabbed Length of Frame Cover

11 Use tacky glue to secure the tabbed length of the frame cover, wrapping the tabs around the corners of the frame. Cut a little slit and glue the overlapping edges down into place.

12 Trim the finishing edges and glue into position.

Glue Finishing Edges into Position

Final Frame

13 Coat the cover using a glue stick. Make sure you do not leave a portion of the chipboard unglued.

Coat Cover with Glue Stick

14 Place the cover in the center of the decorative paper and glue it down. Flip it over, smooth it, and use the heat from your hands to help dry the glue. Along the edges of the cover, make a crease in the decorative paper between two fingers. This will make the edges of your book look extra sharp.

Adhere Cover to Decorative Paper

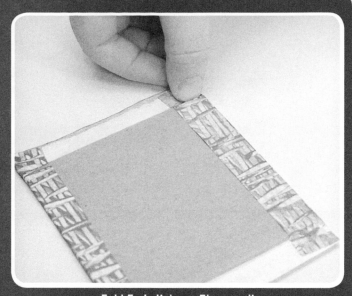

Fold Ends Using a Fingernail

15 Glue down the two opposite edges and use your fingernail or a bone folder to really fold down the ends that will be turned under.

Pinch Corners and Fold

16 When you pinch the corners in, be sure to keep the edges of the paper a little off the edges of the cover as shown. If you pull the fold in too close, it will make a bulky corner. Remember that there are no right or wrong corner-folding methods, just good choices for the materials involved. You may want to use a different corner method if your cover material is too thick to make a relatively flat one using this technique.

Measure Tape

17 Cut a strip of tape a little longer than the board and lay it sticky side up. Place the covers about ⅞" apart, putting an equal amount of tape on either side. Sometimes it's easier to line up the tape and boards on a cutting mat with gridlines. To determine the width of the spine tape, you must consider the depth of your frame piece and add about ⅜" to allow for the added thickness of your chipboard and tape.

18 Fold the excess tape edges down, making sure that you do not close up the spine width by taping straight across. You must ease the tape ends down into the valley and crease it to the inside of the cover board edge.

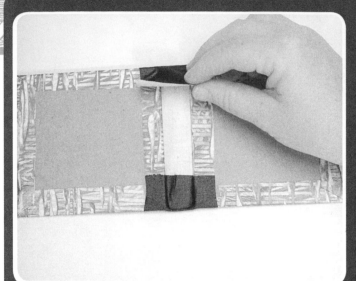

Fold Tape Ends

19 Cut a piece of tape slightly shorter than the covers and lay it down, starting on one side and creasing it in towards the cover edge as shown.

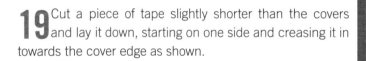

Cut Tape and Crease Towards Cover Edge

20 Continue laying the tape down into the valley, creasing as you go. A straight fold across will close up the spine width, so be careful.

Continue Laying Tape into Valley

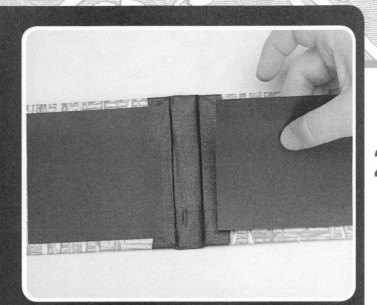

Glue Liner Papers

21 Glue the liner papers into place on the front and back covers.

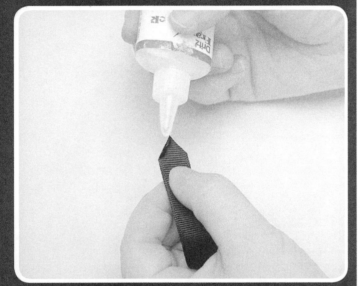

Use Fray Check

22 Use Fray Check to finish the edge of the little strip of ribbon for the hangtag. This is the little tab you may want to insert so that you can pin your display items onto it. This is an optional step.

Glue Tab into Position

23 Use white glue to place the tab into position.

Continues

24 Use a black felt-tip pen to hide any unsightly white edges that may show on your tape.

Use Pen to Hide White Edges

25 Use tacky glue for good adhesion of the frame to the back cover board.

Glue Frame to Back Cover Board

26 Fold the wrapper (in this case, the longer ribbon) onto the D-ring and secure it with a dab of white glue. Cut a tiny slit and insert the eyelet. Remember not to go wild with the blade—the opening has to be small enough only to hold the eyelet.

Fold Wrapper onto D-Ring

Set Eyelet with Setter

27 Set the eyelet with the setter. Finish the pointed edge of the ribbon with Fray Check.

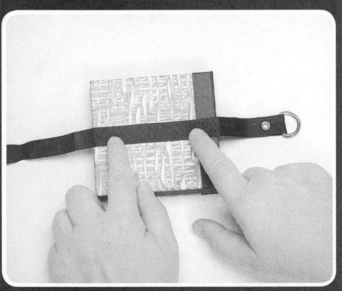

Apply Tacky Glue to Ribbon Wrap

28 Use the tacky glue to adhere the ribbon wrap to the backside of the book.

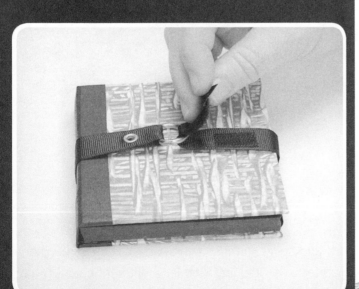

Bring Wrap Around and Thread Through D-Ring

29 Bring the wrap around, thread it through the D-ring for the correct position, and then adhere the self-stick pieces of hook-and-loop tape.

Frame of Gold

This is a fun craft to do to make wood look like metal. The gold leafing is heated to create interesting colors and textures. Experiment with gold leafing and other plastic objects.

 Must-Haves: Materials

Flat wooden frame • Lizard and spiral stamps • Ink pad, black • Dimensional Magic, any color • Spray adhesive • Gold leaf sheets: 2 different colors or patterns • Soft cloth • Heat tool • Gold paint (optional)

Squeeze Dimensional Magic Onto Design

1 Stamp your images onto the frame using black ink. Heat-set the ink for two minutes.

2 Squeeze Dimensional Magic onto the design to give a raised texture.

Allow to Dry

3 Allow to dry for several hours.

Spray Adhesive

4 Spray adhesive to the front and sides of the frame. Allow to dry for ten minutes.

Continues

5 Carefully lay sheets of gold leaf onto the frame. Cover all areas using two different colors or patterns of gold leaf.

6 Rub the entire frame with a soft cloth. Make sure you hold the frame over a shallow box or something that can catch extra bits of the leaf.

Lay Sheets of Gold Leaf

7 Using the black ink pad, rub over raised stamp areas to create contrast.

Use Black Ink Pad

8 Heat-set inked areas. Paint the back of the frame with gold paint if desired, or cover with more gold leaf.

Heat Inked Areas

Fantastic Fabric Accessories

These pins are a great project that you can make as simple or as complex as you wish. Use your imagination and add in your own special touches!

 Must-Haves: Materials

Natural muslin (enough for the fronts and backs of your pins) • Stamps • One black Fabrico ink pad • Heat tool • Assorted fabric paints and paintbrushes • Needle and black thread or a sewing machine threaded with black thread • Black permanent ink pen • Scissors • Embellishments (assorted beads, metallic fibers, charms, mounting boards) • Fray Check • Skewer • Stuffing material • Tacky glue • Pinback

1 Stamp your image in black Fabrico ink. Use your heat gun to set the ink, readying it for watercolors.

Stamp Image

2 Paint the image with fabric paints. To avoid obscuring the stamped lines, you may need to thin the paints a little. Createx and Ready Tex are sheer enough to let the stamped lines show through, but Polymark and Tulip paints will need to be thinned with water.

Paint Image

3 Use a wide brush to paint coordinating fabric paints on the material for the back of the pin. Lavender and orange fabric paint are shown here. Gold metallic fabric paint was added next. Use your heat gun to speed the drying process.

Apply Paint to Fabric

4 Stamp a pattern in black Fabrico ink all over and set with a heat gun.

Stamp Pattern All Over

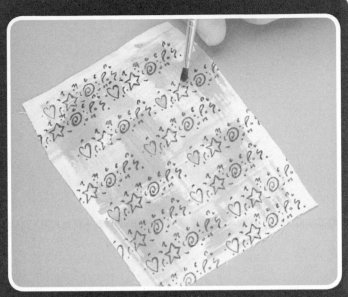

Color Stamped Images

5 Use a smaller paintbrush to color the stamped images with fabric paint.

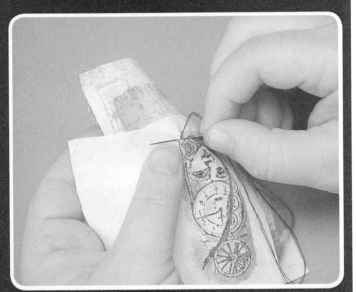

Sew Pieces Together

6 Choose a spot on the decorative backing fabric. Position the front piece over it, so that the decorated sides of both pieces of fabric face outward. Sew the two pieces together with tiny stitches. With the right side of both pieces facing outward, you won't have to turn these pins right side out after sewing them.

Use Black Permanent Ink Pen

7 You may want to use a black permanent ink pen to redraw the lines if they have been covered with paint. Choose a pen that will be both waterproof and bleedproof on the fabric.

8 Use a sharp pair of scissors to cut out the pin, leaving about a ⅛" margin all around the sewn edge. The pin can remain as it is, or you can embellish it further with beads, fibers, and charms.

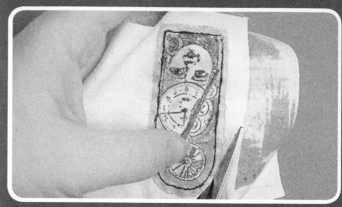

Cut Out Pin

9 Apply Fray Check on the raw edges to prevent raveling of the fabric. Allow to dry naturally, or use a heat gun to hurry up the drying.

Apply Fray Check

10 Pinch the pin so that the back pops up to make it easier to cut a slit for the filling.

Cut Slit for Filling

11 Use a skewer to push tiny amounts of filler into the pin until it is stuffed to a nice level.

Use Skewer to Stuff

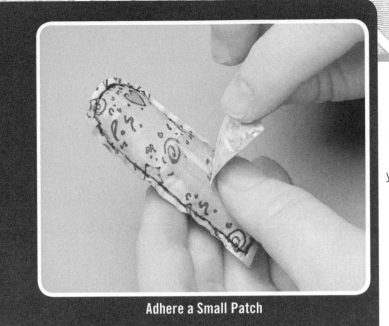

Adhere a Small Patch

12 Use white tacky glue to adhere a small patch of fabric over the filler opening. Sew or glue a small pinback to your project.

This little pin was embellished with beads and metallic thread. The headdress is one-half of a brass-colored hanger from a Christmas tree bulb. You can flatten them out and burn them to get rid of the brass color, creating an "aged" look.

This pin's second image was cut out to reveal only the flower portion. The flower was treated using the same techniques as the main pin and then attached with tacky glue. A decorative button was glued onto the flower. Colored beads were added to the overall piece by using Polymark dimensional fabric paint. A beaded ornament was attached to the bottom of the pin with a gold jump ring.

Beads of Beauty

Beads have a wide variety of uses in the world of arts and crafts. The most obvious is jewelry, but you can also use your beads glued to the bottom of boxes for feet, glued to the top for handles, strung onto sling handles and in assemblage. Fancy fibers threaded through the large beads make wonderful tassels.

 Must-Haves: Materials

Wooden beads of any size and shape • Fine-grit sandpaper • Stamps • Black waterproof ink pad • One sheet of white drawing paper • Perfect Paper Adhesive • Paintbrush for use with glue • Stipple brush • Straw-colored ink pad • Colored pencils • Watercolors (optional) • Skewer • Clear sealant • Gloss coating (Crystal Cote makes a thick, shiny glaze, but clear nail polish works as well)

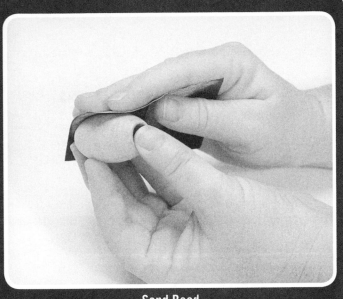

Sand Bead

1 Sand the glossy finish off the bead.

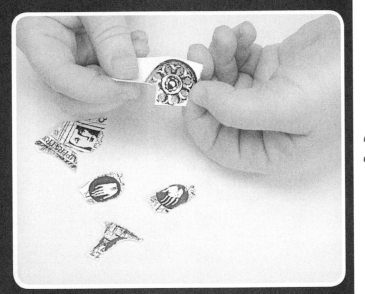

Stamp Images in Ink

2 Stamp images in black waterproof ink and tear out.

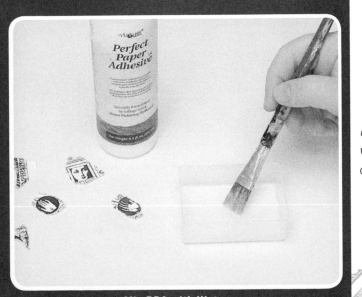

Mix PPA with Water

3 Put a little Perfect Paper Adhesive (PPA) in a small container and dilute it with water so that it is of the same consistency as thick cream.

Continues

4 Use the glue brush to apply a coat of PPA to the bead, then apply a coat of PPA to the back side of the paper.

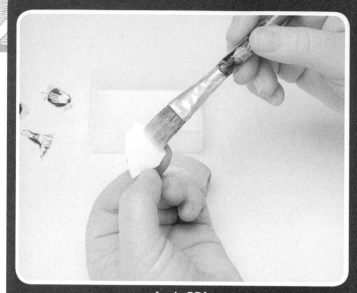

Apply PPA

5 Position the paper onto the bead and affix it with another coat of PPA on top of the paper.

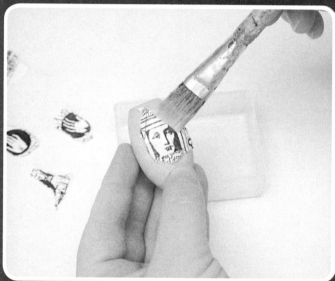

Position and Affix Paper

6 You can use the brush alone to smooth down the wrinkled paper for good adhesion, but I prefer to use my hands to really mold the paper to the curved surface of the bead. The PPA is not sticky at all—it feels like hand cream, so it's perfect for applications like this.

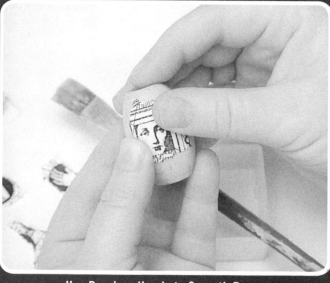

Use Brush or Hands to Smooth Paper

Continuing Affixing Paper

7 Continue covering the bead with pieces of stamped paper.

Use Stipple Brush

8 When the glue is dry, use the stipple brush to apply a straw color to various degrees. Remember to stamp a little color off the brush onto scratch paper before applying it directly to the stamped image. This will avoid any big splotches of ink that are darker and more spotty than intended.

Use Colored Pencils

9 Use the colored pencils to color your images.

10 Thread the bead onto a skewer and spray it with a clear sealant. (If you don't, the stippled dye inks may run under the final gloss coat.)

Spray with Clear Sealant

11 Brush or spray a glossy finish onto your bead.

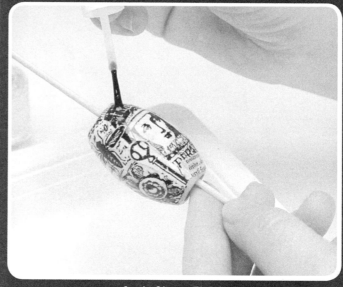

Apply Glossy Finish

This pretty bead started with black paper that was stamped and embossed in gold.

After adhering the pieces of paper onto the bead, metallic pens were used to color it. The colors were set with a spray sealant, then two coats of the Crystal Cote glossy finish were applied.

Another option is to paint the bead with acrylic paint, then emboss it with a variety of colored embossing powders.

Fancy Fabric Note Cover

Why not decorate an old notebook that's been lying around with a gorgeous rubber-stamped cover? Choose a pretty, muted fabric pattern to make sure that your rubber stamp pattern shows up well. The finished project's size can vary so that its finished look can house an array of things: makeup pouches, pencil cases—you name it!

Must-Haves: Materials

Pen and notepad • Fabric for front and back of notebook • Fusible webbing and stiff fusible interfacing • Iron • Cutting mat • Rotary Cutter • Straightedge • Stamps of your choice • Sponge brush • Apple Barrel matte acrylic paints • FolkArt metallic paints • Fabri-Tac Glue • 18" braid, about ½ yard • Scissors • Piece of wire • Needle-nosed pliers • Button

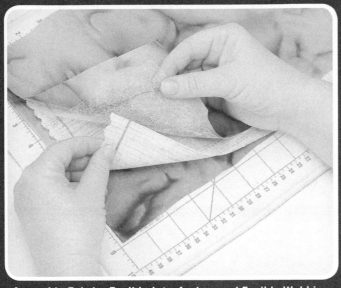

Assemble Fabric, Fusible Interfacing, and Fusible Webbing

1 Cut two pieces of fabric—one for the front cover and one for the back, one piece of stiff, fusible interfacing, and one piece of fusible webbing. Assemble them as shown, with the right sides of the fabric facing outward. The fusible interfacing has the fusing material on one side only. You'll need the extra webbing to fuse the layers together. Iron flat.

Line Up Fabric Packet on Cutting Mat

2 After the fabric pack has cooled, line it up on the grid of a cutting mat. Trim to size and shape you prefer, using a rotary cutter and straightedge. Cut the fabric so the folder extends 1' over the top and bottom of the notepad. It should be twice the width of the pad, plus allow about 1" for the pen and about 2" for the front flap.

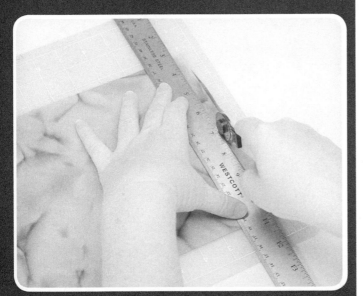

3 Use a sponge brush to dab acrylic paint onto a stamp. A light matte color, like yellow or white acrylic paint, will add opacity to the metallic paint.

Use Sponge Brush to Apply Acrylic Paint on Stamp

Continues

4 Stamp randomly over fabric in a variety of colors.

Stamp Randomly

5 Apply glue along the edge of the cover. Position the braid so that it will fold over to cover the raw edges of the fabric. Glue it down on one side. Then, flip it over and glue the braid down on the other side.

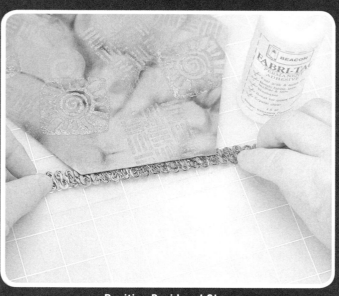

Position Braid and Glue

6 Cut a piece of braid a little wider than the notepad. Slide the braid under a few of the last pages for positioning. Fold the ends of the braid under and glue into position.

Fold Ends of Braid Under

Size the Pen Holder

7 For easy sizing for the pen holder, snugly wrap the pen with a piece of braid and glue one end over the other. Be careful not to glue the pen to the braid.

Apply Glue to Overlapped Braid

8 Place a dab of glue on the overlapped braid and hold the pen assembly in place until the glue sets.

Tips & Quips: Fabric glue dries quickly, but for extra speed, a glue gun can be used in place of Fabri-Tac.

Stick Curled Ends Through a Button and Fabric

9 Curl the ends of a piece of wire with pliers, then stick it through a button and the fabric.

Tie Cord End Around Button

10 Tie one end of the cord around the button. The closure is a simple wrap.

Resources

Stamps

Acey Deucy
P.O. Box 194
Ancram, NY 12502

American Art Stamp
3892 Del Amo Bld.
Ste. 701
Torrance, CA 90503
www.americanartstamp.com

ArtSeeds.com
P.O. Box 37041
Tucson, AZ 85740
(520) 219-0407
www.artseeds.com

Claudia Rose
15 Baumgarten
Saugerties, NY 12477

Creative Black/Stamper Anonymous
20613 Center Ridge Rd.
Rocky River, OH 44116
www.stampersanony
mous.com

ERA Graphics
2476 Ottawa Way
San Jose, CA 95130
(408) 364-1124
www.eragraphics.com

Hero Arts
1343 Powell St.
Emeryville, CA 94608
www.heroarts.com

Impress Me Rubber Stamps
17116 Escalon Drive
Encino, CA 91436-4030

JudiKins
17803 S. Harvard Blvd.
Gardena, CA 90248
www.judi-kins.com

Kodomo No Kao Co. Ltd.
4-6-2 Higashi-
nakano Nakano
Tokyo, Japan
011-81-3-3360-9806

Magenta Rubber Stamps
351 Rue Blain
Mont Saint Hilarie
Quebec J3H3B4
Canada
www.magentarub-
berstamps.com

Out West
P.O. Box 6921
Apache Junction, AZ 85278
(480) 288-5800

Personal Stamp Exchange
360 Sutton Place
Santa Rosa, CA 95407
(707) 588-8058
www.homesweetzone.com

Posh Impressions
22600-A Lambert St.
Ste. 706
Lake Forest, CA 92630
www.poshimpressions.com

Print Blocks
1/81 Bishop Street
Kelvin Grove
Brisbane QLD 4059
Australia
(07) 3356 7933

Rubber Moon
P.O. Box 3258
Hayden Lake, ID 83835

Rubber Stampede
2550 Pellissier Place
Whittier, CA 90601
(800) 623-8386

Stamp Francisco
Coco Stamp
1248 Ninth Ave.
San Francisco, CA 94122

Stampington & Company
22992 Mill Creek Dr.
Ste. B
Laguna Hills, CA 92653
www.stampington.com

Stephanie Olin's Rubber Stamps
6171 Foxshield Dr.
Huntington Beach,
CA 92647

Tin Can Mail
c/o Stamp Rosa
6 Maxwell Court
Santa Rosa, CA 95401
(800)554-5755
www.stamparosa.com

Uptown Design Co.
10 Caledonia Summit
Bowns Pont, WA 98422
(800) 888-3212
(253) 925-1234
www.uptowndesign.com

Zettiology
P.O. Box 2665
Renton, WA 98056

Other Supplies

Artistic Wire Ltd.
752 N. Larch Avenue
Elmhurst, IL 60126
(630) 530-7567
www.artisticwire.com

Binney & Smith, Inc.
100 Church Lane
Easton, PA 18044
www.binney-smith.com

Chemtek
(888) 871-8100
www.chemtek.com

Clearsnap, Inc.
Box 98
Anacortes, WA 98221
(800) 448-4862
(360) 293-6634
www.clearsnap.com

Fascinating Folds
P.O. Box 10070
Glendale, AZ 85318
(800) 968-2418
(602) 375-9908
www.fascinatingfolds.com

Fiskars, Inc.
7811 W. Stewart Ave.
Wausau, WI 54401
www.fiskars.com

Lenderink Technologies
P.O. Box 310
Belmont, MI 49306
(616) 887-8257

Marvy-Uchida
3535 Del Amo Blvd.
Torrance, CA 90503
www.uchida. com

Nasco Arts & Crafts
4825 Stoddard Rd.
Modesto, CA 95356
(800) 558-9595

Ranger Industries
15 Park Road
Tinton Falls, NJ 07724
(732) 389-3535
www.rangerink.com

Rupert, Gibbon & Spider, Inc.
P.O. Box 425
Healdsburg, CA 95448
(800) 442-0455
www.jacquardproducts.com

ScottiCrafts
Mount Vernon, NY
www.scotticrafts.com

SDK Distributors
P.O. Box 421
Marlboro, NJ 07746
(800) 546-8641

Suze Weinberg Design Studio
39 Old Bridge Dr.
Howell, NJ 07731
www.schmoozewithsuze.com

Tsukineko
15411 N.E. Ninety-fifth St.
Redmond, WA 98052
www.tsukineko.com

US ArtQuest, Inc.
7800 Ann Arbor Rd.
Grass Lake, MI 49240
www.usartquest.com

VIP
1215 N. Grove St.
Anaheim, CA 92806

Acknowledgments

A very special thanks to those who contributed
projects for this publication, especially:

Sandra McCall, for the following projects:

Personal Portfolio, page 26

The Perfect Pin, page 31

Fancy Folio, page 40

Light Up My Life Lampshade, page 50

Tiny Tassel Book, page 61

Tiny Treasure Box, page 75

Key to My Art, page 78

Marvelous Memories Book, page 88

Idea Box, page 92

Precious Push-Pins, page 103

Designer Display Kit, page 115

Fantastic Fabric Accessories, page 129

Beads of Beauty, page 134

Vesta Abel, for the following projects:

Handy Light, page 37

I'll Give You My Heart Box, page 45

Paperback Protector, page 55

Candle Décor, page 71

Metal Décor, page 82

Classy Clay Charm, page 100

Terrific Trinket Box, page 108

Frame of Gold, page 126

Index

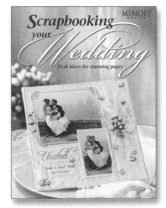

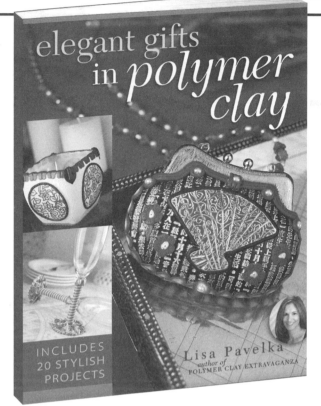

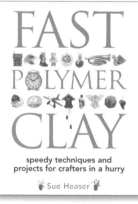
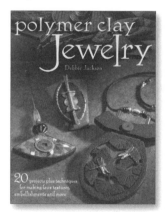

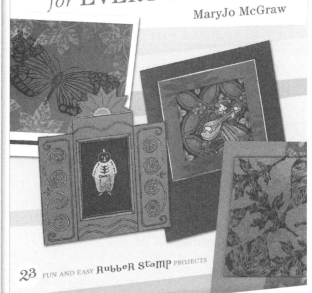

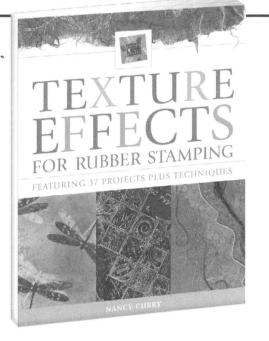

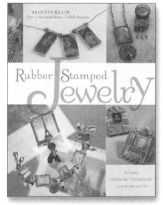

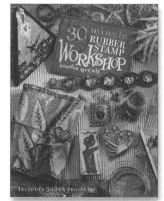